PUNK LITERATURE

Books LLC®, Wiki Series, Memphis, USA, 2011. ISBN: 9781158202263. www.booksllc.net
Copyright: http://creativecommons.org/licenses/by-sa/3.0/deed.en

Table of Contents

Punk comics
Ariel Schrag 1
Books of Magick: Life During Wartime 2
Cristy Road 4
East Coast Rising 5
Fly (artist) 5
Ghost World 5
Kill Your Boyfriend 8
Love and Rockets (comics) 9
Nothing Nice to Say 12
Peter Pank 14
Tank Girl 14
The Invisibles 17

Punk literature
DJ DB 20
Punk literature 21
The Encyclopedia of Punk 21

Punk writers
Diablo Cody 22
Kathy Acker 23

Punk zines
Aaron Cometbus 26
Absolutely Zippo 27
Black Market Magazine 27
Burnt Offering 28
Chainsaw (punk zine) 28
Death To The World 28
Flipside (fanzine) 29
Homocore (zine) 29
J.D.s 30
Jamming (fanzine) 30
KCDIY 31
Kill Your Pet Puppy 31
Maximumrocknroll 31

No Cure 32
Peroxide (punk zine) 32
Profane Existence 33
Punk (magazine) 34
Punk Globe 34
Punk Planet 35
Punk zine 35
Razorcake 36
Rolling Thunder (journal) 37
Slash (fanzine) 37
Slug and Lettuce (fanzine) 38
Sluggo! 39
Sniffin' Glue 39
Suburban Voice 40
The Positives 40
Touch and Go: The Complete Hardcore Punk Zine '79-'83" 40
Verbicide Magazine 41

Introduction

Purchase of this book entitles you to a free trial membership in the publisher's book club at www.booksllc.net. (Time limited offer.) Simply enter the barcode number from the back cover onto the membership form. The book club entitles you to select from hundreds of thousands of books at no additional charge. You can also download a digital copy of this and related books to read on the go. Simply enter the title or subject onto the search form to find them.

Each chapter in this book ends with a URL to a hyperlinked online version. Type the URL exactly as it appears. If you change the URL's capitalization it won't work. Use the online version to access related pages, websites, footnotes, tables, color photos, updates. Click the version history tab to see the chapter's contributors. Click the edit link to suggest changes.

A large and diverse editor base collaboratively wrote the book, not a single author. After a long process of discussion and debate, the chapters gradually took on a neutral point of view reached through consensus. Additional editors expanded and contributed to chapters striving to achieve balance and comprehensive coverage. This reduced the regional or cultural bias found in many other books and provided access and breadth on subject matter otherwise little documented.

Ariel Schrag

Ariel Schrag (b. December 29, 1979, in Berkeley, California) is an American cartoonist and television writer who achieved critical recognition at an unusually early age for her autobiographical comics.

Biography
While attending high school in Berkeley, California, Schrag self-published her first comic series, *Awkward*, depicting events from her freshman year, originally selling copies to friends and family. Slave Labor Graphics subsequently reprinted *Awkward* as a graphic novel, followed by three more books based on her next three years of school: *Definition, Potential,* and *Likewise*. The books were republished by Touchstone/Simon & Schuster in 2008 and 2009. The books tell stories of family life, going to concerts, experimenting with drugs, high school crushes, and coming out as

a bisexual and later as a lesbian.

Schrag was nominated for the 1998 Kimberly Yale Award for Best New Talent (administered by the Friends of Lulu).

Killer Films is producing a movie adaptation of *Potential*; Schrag has written the screenplay.

Schrag graduated from Berkeley High School in 1998. She graduated from Columbia University with a bachelor's degree in English in 2003, and has continued to work as a cartoonist.

The documentary *Confession: A Film About Ariel Schrag* was released in 2004. It explores the then-23-year-old Schrag's world in which she "negotiates fame, obsesses about disease, and discusses the way she sees as a dyke comic book artist."

Schrag was a writer for the third and fourth seasons of the Showtime series *The L Word'*".

Schrag is currently a writer for the HBO series *How To Make It In America*.

Schrag lives in Brooklyn, NY.

In popular culture

Schrag was listed in *The Advocate's* list of "Forty under Forty" out media professionals in its June–July 2009 issue.
Source (edited): "http://en.wikipedia.org/wiki/Ariel_Schrag"

Books of Magick: Life During Wartime

Books of Magick: Life During Wartime is a fantasy comic book series published by DC Comics under their Vertigo imprint in 2004 and 2005 that was discontinued after fifteen issues.

All of the issues are written by Si Spencer, with some script consultation done by Neil Gaiman. The artwork is done solo by Dean Ormston throughout most of the series' run. Steve Yeowell is co-credited as an artist in issues eleven and twelve and Duncan Fegredo fully replaces Ormston for issues six and ten.

The series depicts the events that take place on two fictional worlds, both of which are connected through an alternate version of the character Timothy Hunter.

When Timothy Hunter first appeared he was a young boy who had the potential to be the world's most powerful magic user. He starred in his own series titled *The Books of Magic*. Over the course of the character's history he changed and aged.

The idea behind *Books of Magick: Life During Wartime* was to present a more mature version of *The Books of Magic* without the character's past continuity attached. During the planning stage a problem appeared. A series of books based on the comics and also titled *The Books of Magic* had been released and marketed in this form to children. *Books of Magick: Life During Wartime* depicts nudity and sex, as well as a higher degree of violence than *The Books of Magic*. Although tastefully depicted these things make it a series inappropriate for children and there were fears that the new series and the books could be confused in some sectors. The decision to change 'Magic' to 'Magick' and to add the words 'Life During Wartime' was made and the series went forward.

Setting

The true Earth of this series is a world upon which humans (known as the Bred) live side-by-side with members of the races of Faerie (known as the Born). It is a world torn by war. On one side is the ruling elite made exclusively of Born. On the other is the Coalition made up of both Born and Bred. The majority on both sides are members of the same religion. They worship Tim Hunter as a god under the name The Hunter.

The second Earth is known as Hunter's World and was created by Hunter as a means of protection and escape. The things he was running from were magic, war, and religion. As a result when he created Hunter's World none of those things existed there.

Publication history

The first five issues detail the current status quo in the final days of the war. The Born make their final attack and the war ends in issues seven to nine. Issues eleven to fifteen show the aftermath of these events with eleven and twelve dealing with the true Earth and thirteen, fourteen and fifteen showing the fate of Hunter's World and the main cast of characters. These three sections are separated by two one issue stories that show events from the perspective of two supporting characters. Issue six shows Dog's perspective while issue ten deals with Cat's.

Although it was never solicited as such, *Books of Magick: Life During Wartime* was planned as a limited series as many Vertigo series are.

Characters

- **Tim Hunter** - The most powerful magic user on the real Earth. He is worshiped as a god, but hates it. He only wants the war to stop.
- **John Constantine and Zatanna** - They are two of Tim's closest friends and key players around which events move. These two characters are based on the DC Universe characters of the same names (see John Constantine and Zatanna).
- **Molly** - She is Tim's girlfriend on Hunter's World.
- **Cat and Dog** - They are brother and sister and Tim's close friends on Hunter's World.
- **Brewster** - He is the only other person living on Hunter's World not created by Tim. His mission is to safeguard Tim for the Coalition and to ensure his memory of the real world returns when it needs to.
- **Lord Midian** - A Faerie and one of the leaders of Coalition. He is in charge of the Coalition's Navy.
- **The Faerie Queen** - She is the leader of the Born and rules over Earth from her palace in Jerusalem.

Plot synopsis

The Beginning of the End

The series starts fifteen months into the war between the Born and the Coalition.

On the real world John Constantine finds himself in charge of the besieged city of Kraków. The forces inside are surrounded by the soldiers of the Born under the command of a monstrous Faerie known as The Cherish, and the food stores ran out seven months previously. In Jerusalem Zatanna searches for a way to obtain the three keys that will give her access to the Books of Magick. Her hope is that the books will allow Tim Hunter to regain all of his memories when he comes back from his exile.

Things get worse for the Coalition when an apparition of the Hunter appears worldwide. Seeing this the Coalition launches its naval fleet from Reykjavík to attack England (known as Albion on this world) despite the misgiving of Lord Midian. This turns out to be a disastrous move when the fleet is destroyed by giant wood golems guarding the landing beaches. In Kraków things get much worse when the forces surrounding the city begin launching deadly cluster spells. On top of all of this Zatanna is captured in Jerusalem and tortured. The pain of this last event is lessened when Zatanna escapes taking the three keys to the Books of Magick with her. The apparition also allows the Faerie Queen to discover Tim's location. She sends her agents, the Micturides to get him.

On Hunter's World, Tim meets his girlfriend Molly at the train station. Later they meet with their friends Cat and Dog who give Tim a book named *The Books of Magick*. After looking through it he collapses and sees a vision of the real world. While in the middle of this vision he inadvertently causes the apparition that appeared there.

This event causes Brewster to make his presence known. He introduces himself a few days later and enters Tim's circle of friends. Brewster begins to take actions that are designed to force Tim to use his powers and to remember magic again.

Strange things begin to happen around Tim at this point. These culminate when Cat collapses one day. Her eyes turn solid red and insects begin to exit her mouth. Tim drives to the oceanside and submerges her and himself in the water. The magic he uses in this location allows him to save her. While this is going on The Micturides arrive and are confronted by Brewster.

The Return of the Hunter

On the true Earth things are dark for the Coalition. The Born begin their invasion of Iceland (known as Thule on this world and the last nation still under Coalition control).

On Hunter's World Tim has regained enough of his memories to know who he is and where he comes from. He creates a church and has a funeral for Brewster who he believes was killed by the Micturides. In attendance are the very confused Molly, Cat and Dog. A very much still living Brewster arrives and begins to argue with Tim over Tim's actions. The argument grows heated and Tim's church is cracked in half. In the chaos Molly, Cat and Dog disappear only to appear in the real world. Molly appears to John Constantine in Kraków. Dog appears in Zatanna's shower in Jerusalem while she is taking a shower. Finally, Cat appears in front of a captured Lord Midian in Thule and is taken prisoner alongside the other Coalition survivors.

The War Ends

The Cherish on the cover of issue #9. Art by Frank Quitely

Tim arrives back in the real world along with Brewster. While deciding what to do they encounter a group of Alfar, a Faerie race known for eating other sentients. Tim begins a relationship with one of their women named Birgit. After coming to a decision on what his actions should be Tim transports his allies to the prison in Thule where Cat and Midian are being held. They rescue Cat but Midian dies from wounds he received while being tortured.

While Tim is in Thule, The Cherish gives the order to begin the final assault on Kraków. Tim and his allies teleport in not long after that order is given. In the battle Birgit is killed and Tim challenges the Cherish to one on one combat. The head of the Cherish's conjoined twin is cut off by one of her own soldiers just as she is about to kill Tim. This soldier is a worshiper of the Hunter and did not wish to see his god killed. This small victory is not enough to save the day as the forces of the Born overwhelm the city's defenders and the war comes to a conclusion.

Confronting the Queen

Tim, Molly, Constantine and Cat are taken as prisoners to Jerusalem where they are placed in chains at the head of a victory parade led by The Cherish. The spectacle winds its way through the streets on its way to the Queen's palace.

Seeing this Zatanna and Dog hatch a plan to steal the last of the Books of Magick. Slipping into the palace they quickly make their way to the room containing the last book. Just as they are about to take the book the soldiers assigned to guard the book discover their presence.

In the Queen's throne room, Tim and his allies are presented to the Queen. Tim casts an illusionary spell that distracts the Queen long enough to allow an escape. Constantine leads this small group through the palace halls to where Zatanna and Dog are fighting. Now joined together, Tim and his allies take the last of the books and fight their way to a place of temporary safety. There Tim assembles all four books and casts the spell that will give him all of his memories back.

The spell fails and the Faerie Queen appears in the doorway. John Constantine goes to her and they embrace. He reveals that he is her lover, that he has been working for the Born the entire time and that the two of them destroyed the true Books of Magick months previously. As The Queen prepares to kill Tim and end any threat to her reign, Tim joins hands with Molly, Cat and Dog and casts a spell. Tim's three friends from Hunter's World crumble before his eyes and disappear. The effect on the Faerie Queen is similar as she dies and takes on the appearance of a desiccated corpse.

Seeking to see the Queen's true appearance Zatanna turns the corpse over only to see a feminine version of Tim's face. Constantine reveals that she was an alternate version of Tim and both he and Zatanna reveal to Tim that Constantine's actions were a double cross. Constantine's plan was to trick the Queen into allowing a small group close enough that she could be killed.

The Final Fate of Hunter's World

Since Tim's return to the true world, the social situation on Hunter's World has deteriorated. Tim returns with Brewster and is shocked to find that the strange events that preceded his departure have caused a religion to form. In a reflection of the true world this religion worships Tim as a deity under the name The Hunter.

This world has its own version of John Constantine named Jackie Constantine. We meet her in her job as a delivery girl. Her assignment is to take a small package to the church that Tim created. Since Tim's leavetaking it has become the center of the new religion and the home for its leaders, the Holy Six. Jackie's delivery goes wrong and she barely gets away with her life.

Jackie is fired and now jobless she rescues a young woman from Hunter worshippers who were about to burn her at the stake. The young woman's name is Charlotte and the two of them become lovers. Later Jackie encounters a woman running from some more Hunter worshippers and saves her as well. This woman turns out to be the woman that Tim created on Hunter's World to be his "mother." This rescue leads to an encounter with Molly, Dog and Cat who have recently reappeared back on Hunter's World. The three of them and Brewster have a mission for her.

Tim has decided to destroy Hunter's World and Jackie is sent to talk to him in hopes that she can talk him out of it. She fails at this and Hunter's World ceases to exist. The only survivors are Jackie, Charlotte, Tim's "Mother," Dog, Cat and Molly. Along with Brewster, Tim transports this group to another realm using two cabins from the Hunter's World version of the London Eye.

This new world is a place of lush green beauty free from predators. Tim tells Cat and Dog that they are not really brother and sister and that they will be this dimension's Adam and Eve.

Tim takes the rest of his group to the Realm of Faerie to drop off Brewster and to have a talk with Titania, the Queen of Faerie (not to be confused with the foe he defeated). Molly and Tim's "mother" wander, see what Faerie is like and decide to stay.

Jackie and Charlotte travel with Tim to the true Earth. There Tim uses his powers to set them up in a new life. Although most of the reviews were favorable, there was some criticism. Most of this centered around the thought that, despite the fact that the story had no connection to the past history of Timothy Hunter, you still needed to know that history to fully understand many plot details. A common comment was "The writers seem to assume that the reader will be familiar with Tim's history."

Collected editions

There has been one trade paperback collection so far:
- *Books of Magick: Life During Wartime: Book 1* (with Dean Ormston, Vertigo, tpb collects #1-5, 2005, ISBN 1401204880)

Source (edited): "http://en.wikipedia.org/wiki/Books_of_Magick:_Life_During_Wartime"

Cristy Road

Cristy C. Road (born May 26, 1982 in Miami, Florida) is an American illustrator of Cuban descent. Blending social principles, sexual deviance, mental inadequacies, and social justice- she thrives to testify the beauty of the imperfect. Her obsession with making art accessible began when publishing GREEN'ZINE in 1996- a fanzine entirely devoted to Green Day. Eventually she began including blurbs on other punk rock bands, gender identity, masturbation, sexuality, aimless travel, and anarchist organizing. Today, Road has moved onto illustrated novels, taking both writing and visual elements a step more seriously, her visual diagram of lifestyles and beliefs stay in tune to the zine's portrayal of living.

In early 2006, Road released an anomalous illustrated storybook, entitled INDESTRUCTIBLE (Microcosm Publishing). It's a 96-page narrative about her experience as a teenager, where Road tackles the themes of being Latina, class, rebellion, gender, queerness, mental health, and death; all beneath the topical umbrella of being a teenage Floridian punk rocker in the early 90's. Road has recently completed a Collection of postcards featuring art from 2001-2007, entitled DISTANCE MAKES THE HEART GROW SICK (Microcosm Publishing). Road just released BAD HABITS (Soft Skull Press), an Illustrated love story about a faltering human heart's telepathic connections to the destruction of New York City; and getting over an abusive relationship. Road currently is working on paintings, short stories, and her punk band THE HOMEWRECKERS . In 2009 her repertoire consists of ten years of independent publishing, two graphic novels, and countless illustrations for a broad slew of magazines, record album art, concert posters, and political organizations. She lives in Brooklyn, NY.
Source (edited): "http://en.wikipedia.org/wiki/Cristy_Road"

East Coast Rising

East Coast Rising is an American comic book published as original graphic novels by Tokyopop and written and drawn by Becky Cloonan. Done in the style of manga, the comic follows the adventures of punk rock pirates on the East Coast of the United States, in a world where New Jersey has become submerged.

Volumes

- *East Coast Rising* Volume 1 (ISBN 1-59816-468-6; published April 30, 2006)
- *East Coast Rising* Volume 2 (scheduled to be released October 2007)

Source (edited): "http://en.wikipedia.org/wiki/East_Coast_Rising"

Fly (artist)

Fly is a comic book artist and illustrator, whose art has been published in several magazines and fanzines, including *Slug and Lettuce*, *Maximum Rock 'N' Roll*, *World War 3 Illustrated*, *Village Voice*. She is also a former member of New York band God Is My Co-Pilot.

Fly came to work in New York in the late 1980s, and got involved with ABC No Rio, a social center for punks and artists located at 156 Rivington street in New York City's Lower East Side. She is a member of the World War 3 Illustrated collective, and a contributor to the anthology *Juicy Mother*, edited by Jennifer Camper, which was published by Manic D Press in 2007.

In 2003, Fly had an art show held in the Cartoon Art Museum in California. She has also done cover artwork for Hungry March Band, Adeline Records and Geykido Comet Records. Aside from freelance cover artwork, she has printed many photocopy zines of her artwork and published books. In 1998, Fly had her first book, CHRON!IC!RIOTS!PA!SM!, published by Autonomedia. In 2003, she published a graphic novel-style book named *PEOPS*, a collection of portraits and stories about people Fly has met. The book was released by Soft Skull Press, and subtitled "Portraits and Stories of People". In 2006, she was invited as a guest speaker at the Victoria International Arts Symposium. In December this same year, Fly appeared at the Grace Comics showcase alongside Elizabeth Merrick.

Aside from visual arts, Fly also engages in the spoken word and musical collage art of her band Zero Content (named after one of her comic strips) which can be heard on several Geykido Comet Records Compilations. Previously, she played bass and did vocals for several years with Craig Flanagin in the band God Is My Co-Pilot, with which she went on tours in the 1990s.
Source (edited): "http://en.wikipedia.org/wiki/Fly_(artist)"

Ghost World

Ghost World is a comic book written and illustrated by Daniel Clowes. It was originally serialized in issues #11 through #18 (June 1993 to March 1997) of Clowes's comic book series *Eightball*, and was first published in book form in 1997 by Fantagraphics Books. A commercial and critical success, it was very popular with teenage audiences on its initial release and developed into a cult classic. The book has been reprinted in multiple editions and was the basis for the 2001 feature film of the same name.

Ghost World follows the day-to-day lives of best friends Enid Coleslaw and Rebecca Doppelmeyer, two cynical, pseudo-intellectual and intermittently witty teenage girls recently graduated from high school in the early 1990s. They spend their days wandering aimlessly around their unnamed American town, criticizing popular culture and the people they encounter while wondering what they will do for the rest of their days. As the comic progresses and Enid and Rebecca make the transition into adulthood, the two develop tensions and drift apart.

A darkly written comic, with intermittently sombre explorations of friendship and modern life, *Ghost World* has become renowned for its frank treatment of adolescence. The comic's success led to a movie adaptation of the same name, released in 2001 to critical acclaim and numerous nominations, including an Academy Award for Writing Adapted Screenplay, written by Clowes.

Overview

Ghost World takes place in an unnamed town filled with shopping malls, fast food restaurants, and urban sprawl. The town plays a key part in the narrative, as it is constantly mocked and criticized by Enid and Rebecca. As the story progresses, the background changes dramatically. The phrase "Ghost World" is seen by the characters several times, painted or graffitied on garage doors, signs, and billboards for an undeclared reason. An interpretation of the phrase "ghost world" is that it illustrates the fact that today, everyone seems to be living in their own world, thus making the objective world a "ghost" world. The term can also apply to the way in which both Enid and Becky, but especially Enid, are haunted by the past. In the special features of the film adaptation, it is said to refer to the fact that the town's individuality is being encroached upon by franchises that are seen everywhere.

Critical response to *Ghost World* was extensive: many critics praised it for its analysis of teenage life, relationships, and the decay of today's society, while others criticized it for being disconnected and morbid. Some reviews even drew comparisons to J.D. Salinger's *Catcher in the Rye* (1950). *The Village Voice* stated that "Clowes spells out the realities of teen angst as powerfully and authentically as Salinger did in *Catcher in the Rye* for an earlier generation." *The Guardian* praised the strip's illustrations and visuals, saying "it is beautifully drawn, with subtle and convincing storylines. A classic portrait of teenage life" and *Time* magazine called it an "instant classic".

Synopsis

Enid Coleslaw (her father had their surname legally changed from "Cohn" before she was born) and Rebecca (Becky) Doppelmeyer are two cynical, intelligent teenage girls who are best friends in the 1990s. They have recently graduated from high school and spend their days wandering around their unnamed town criticizing pop culture and the people they encounter while wondering what they're going to do with the rest of their lives. They are attracted to boys, in theory, but also unhappily entertain the possibility that they might be lesbians. Their friendship is very close, but as the book goes on tensions between them build, especially over Enid's plans to move away to college. They also have a quiet friend named Josh; throughout the book the two girls enjoy teasing him, but they are also attracted to him and eventually a romantic triangle of sorts forms.

A section in the middle of the story features Clowes (referred to as David Clowes) in a cameo, as a cartoonist that Enid admires and with whom she is infatuated, but finds creepy and a "perv" when she actually sees him. The comic ends with Enid and Rebecca separating; while they speak half-heartedly of "getting together sometime", the easy intimacy they once knew is long gone. Rebecca is now in a relationship with Josh and seems on her way to settling into a "normal" life, while Enid, having failed to get into college, is as much of a misfit as ever and finally leaves town alone to start a new life.

Characters

Enid Coleslaw

Impulsive, cynical and bitter, the strip's lead character drifts through her life without care, criticizing almost everyone she meets. Enid Coleslaw is an 18-year-old teenager, who has recently graduated from her high school, with best friend Rebecca Doppelmeyer. Enid takes an interest in playing pranks on other people, purely for her own benefit, especially a classmate named Josh who may be Enid's love interest. Enid also enjoys anything morbid, forcing Josh to take her to a pornographic store, saying "...Becky and I are dying to go in there, but we can't get any boys to take us..." Clowes said of Enid's character "When I started out I thought of her as this id creature . . . Then I realized halfway through that she was just more vocal than I was, but she has the same kind of confusion, self-doubts and identity issues that I still have -- even though she's 18 and I'm 39!".

Enid's eventual fate in *Ghost World* is not explicitly shown; however, she does pack her bags and leave the city on a bus after her relationship with Rebecca ends. Some readers interpret this final section as a metaphor for suicide. This interpretation can be supported by a few subtle indications in the text: 'Norman' at the bus stop, the cemetery pictured in the table of contents, Enid's hearse for sale, and a panel depicting Enid's father and Carol looking very mournfully at an object not pictured. However, interpretation and significance is ultimately left up to each individual reader. One extratextual factor militating against this interpretation is that Enid (as well as Rebecca) makes a cameo appearance as an old lady in Clowes's *Dan Pussey* collection of comics. Pussey is a self-important, nerdy superhero comics artist, and the book ends in the future as Pussey dies alone and unloved, with Rebecca and Enid as two bitter crones in his rest home going through his possessions. When they discover his stash of "silly books" (comic books), they wonder, "What would a grown man want with such foolishness?"

Enid Coleslaw is also an anagram of "Daniel Clowes."

Rebecca Doppelmeyer

Rebecca Doppelmeyer, the secondary protagonist of *Ghost World* is a far more passive and naive character than Enid, as she has a more mainstream personality – while Enid enjoys more peculiar things in life, Rebecca enjoys things that most teenage girls of her age would take an interest in; for example, she reads a teen magazine (*Sassy*) that was popular among young women in the early to mid 1990s (Enid, while criticising Rebecca for owning the magazine, still peruses it), and is also sexually curious about men, having a crush on Josh. Rebecca spends much of the novel either following Enid, to whom she feels inferior, to places she has become fascinated with or listening to Enid talk about the various ins and outs of her life, usually responding in a uninterested and/or sarcastic manner—in fact, most of the time, her responses have nothing to do with what Enid is talking about. She has no particular aspiration in life, clinging to and obsessing over the past. In the end of the novel, Rebecca matures into a sensible young woman. It is made ambiguous whether she pursued a relationship with Josh.

Minor characters

Beyond Enid and Rebecca, there are many minor and recurring characters in the comic strip:

- Josh, a soft-spoken employee at a self-service convenience store. Both Enid and Rebecca are infatuated with him at different points in the story.
- Melorra, an overachieving, perky and popular classmate of Enid and Rebecca who seems to unexpectedly appear out of the blue wherever Enid and Rebecca may be.
- Bob Skeetes, an astrologer that early in the book is referred to as the "creepy Don Knotts guy."
- Oomi, Rebecca's fragile old grandmother, with whom Rebecca lives.
- Norman, an old man who waits on a bench for a bus that never comes.
- Enid's somewhat effeminate father and his girlfriend Carol, who resurfaces from Enid's past.
- Allen, or "Weird Al", the waiter at the fake 1950s diner called Hubba Hubba (the name is changed to Wowsville in the film).
- John Ellis, an acquaintance of Enid and Becky's, who often associates with them despite their dislike of him. John Ellis is obsessed with stereotypically "morbid" and "offensive" things, such as Nazis, serial killers, child pornography, guns, circus freaks, torture, snuff films, and so forth. He is referred to as having a zine called *Mayhem* which runs stories on these topics.
- Johnny Apeshit, a former punk rocker and heroin addict turned would-be businessman, who is famous among the girls for spray painting the word "anarchy" on Enid's dad's car.
- Naomi, a classmate of Enid and Rebecca, called along with Melorra by Enid, "the junior JAPs of America". Enid tells Naomi the story of her first sexual experience and suggests that the two have a casual friendship.
- Allen Weinstein, the boy with whom Enid had her first sexual experience. He smokes pot, listens to reggae and is interested in counter-culture as a way of rebelling against his wealthy parents.
- The Satanists, a middle-aged satanic couple who eat at the diner Enid frequents, Angel's. They may not actually be satanic, but rather appear that way in Enid's imagination. Enid makes fun of their use of an umbrella in broad daylight (an umbrella can often be used as a sunshade).

History

Ghost World was first conceived in the late 1980s and early 1990s by Daniel Clowes, when he was a teenager. Much of the comic is partially inspired by Clowes's own life, for example, Clowes moved from Los Angeles to San Francisco, and he has said that the town in the story is a visual combination of both places. Most of the novel was not written in chronological order. Clowes began writing *Ghost World* on September 9, 1993, and stated that he created the first chapter without any plans to continue it.

Clowes also credits as having drawn some inspiration from the film The World of Henry Orient, in which two curious young girls stalk a middle-aged man who is having an affair. In the book, Enid and Rebecca are obsessed with various strange people in the neighborhood, including "The Satanists" and a psychic named Bob Skeetes.

Many readers have tried to interpret where the title Ghost World comes from; Clowes has said it comes from something he saw scrawled on a building in his Chicago neighborhood. Some of the references in the book (*Sassy*, etc.) date the book very specifically to the 1990s, which Clowes has said was intentional. He wanted to emulate the way that throwaway cultural references in *The Catcher in the Rye* root the novel in a time and place.

The series was a major departure for Clowes, who had previously populated *Eightball* with considerably more outlandish material. Clowes has said in interviews that he chose two teenage girls for his protagonists partly because he could use them to express his more cynical opinions without readers taking the characters as author surrogates.

Clowes has said he chose the pale blue coloring for the book because he wanted to reflect the experience of walking home in the twilight, when every house has a television on and the living rooms are bathed in a ghostly blue light. He also made various changes to the artwork between the original issues and the book collection, perhaps most notably changing Becky's face early in the story so it more closely matches her appearance at the end.

Differences between the comic book version and the graphic novel

With one exception, in which a small amount of yellow was included, the comics as they originally appeared in *Eightball* employed only two colors; the early chapters were in black and dark blue, then black and a lighter shade of blue later on, and black and light green for the final two chapters. The graphic novel reprint uses this light green and black color scheme throughout.

The character design also changed significantly during the original run of the story, with characters' faces becoming cleaner and less detailed, indicative of a shift in Clowes's changing aesthetic in all his comics, eschewing the minute facial details that had long been one of his trademarks, for more simplified designs. The character of John Ellis, for example, had significant shading and cross-hatching on his face in the original comics, where in the book he has a simpler, uncluttered design. Another striking example is a panel on the second page of the first chapter that shows Rebecca reading a magazine. In the original comic, her eyes and chin are shaded in, her hair reaches her shoulders, and she appears to be scowling. In the graphic novel, this panel was redrawn, softening and lightening Rebecca's features. Enid's appearance was also reworked in this panel, and in several others in the first chapter of the book.

The graphic novel includes five new drawings on the copyright, table of contents, acknowledgments, and other prefatory pages. These new drawings are tableaux of events in the characters' lives that take place prior to the story, including their high school graduation, and a graveyard visit, presumably either for Rebecca's parents (who are never seen or mentioned in the story, though the girl lives with her grandmother) or Enid's mother (who is similarly absent). Interestingly, the graduation scene, which shows the two girls in caps and gowns, and Enid giving the finger, was recreated in the film version.

As with *Like a Velvet Glove Cast in Iron*, the chapters of the story were given names in the novel, and a table of contents was added to reflect this.

Film adaptation

Cover art for *Ghost World*, the 2001 film adaptation starring Thora Birch as Enid (right) and Scarlett Johansson as Rebecca (left)

The book was made into a 2001 movie, *Ghost World*, directed by Terry Zwigoff (also known for his award-winning documentary about underground cartoonist Robert Crumb). Thora Birch played Enid, Scarlett Johansson played Rebecca, and Steve Buscemi played Seymour (a composite character, based on elements from the comic characters of Bob Skeetes and Bearded Windbreaker). Josh was played by Brad Renfro.

Merchandise and spin-off material

A collection of merchandise and spin-off material for *Ghost World* has been sold since its release, some of it still available today. This includes a three alternate versions of dolls of Enid. One is available from Fantagraphics with artwork by Clowes depicting Enid having various adventures, and comes with objects featured in the comic (such as the mask she buys from the pornographic store), another "Little Enid" from the Eightball comic, and an Enid/Rebecca pairing with the likeness of voodoo dolls. The price ranges from US$10–35.

Works influenced

The comic was the influence for Aimee Mann's song "Ghost World" on her album *Bachelor No. 2* (2000).

Collections

- Hardcover Edition: ISBN 1-56097-280-7 Fantagraphics Books (December 1, 1997)
- Paperback Edition: ISBN 1-56097-427-3 Fantagraphics Books; 4th edition (April 1, 2001)
- Paperback Edition: ISBN 1-56097-427-3 Fantagraphics Books; 13th edition (December, 2005)

Source (edited): "http://en.wikipedia.org/wiki/Ghost_World"

Kill Your Boyfriend

Kill Your Boyfriend is the title of a comic book one-shot written by Grant Morrison and drawn by Philip Bond and D'Israeli for DC Comics Vertigo imprint in June 1995.

Publication history

Originally published as part of the Vertigo Voices series of one-shots in 1995, *Kill Your Boyfriend* was reprinted in the prestige format (ISBN 156389453X) in 1998 with an afterword from Morrison and a paper fortune teller. A third edition was published in October 2008.

Synopsis

The story is a darkly comic satire of British youth culture (with hints towards such films as *Natural Born Killers*) which revolves round a bookish middle class schoolgirl, who has a bland unexciting life until she meets a strange young boy who convinces her to kill her boyfriend. They then go on the run together for a series of anarchic adventures across Britain.

Meeting up with a group of travellers in a double-decker bus, the pair indulge in more crime and sexual experimentation before making their way to Blackpool to meet their final fate.

Morrison notes in the afterword of the second edition that the story is inspired in part by the myth of Dionysus.

Source (edited): "http://en.wikipedia.org/wiki/Kill_Your_Boyfriend"

Love and Rockets (comics)

Love and Rockets (often abbreviated *L&R*) is a black and white comic book series by Gilbert Hernandez and Jaime Hernandez, sometimes cited jointly as Los Bros Hernandez. Their brother Mario Hernandez is an occasional contributor. It was one of the first comics in the alternative comics revolution of the 1980s.

Overview

The Hernandez brothers self-published the first issue of Love and Rockets in 1981, but since 1982 it has been published by Fantagraphics Books. The magazine temporarily ceased publication in 1996 after the release of issue #50, while Gilbert and Jaime went on to do separate series involving many of the same characters. However, in 2001 Los Bros revived the series as *Love and Rockets Volume 2*.

Love and Rockets contains several ongoing serial narratives, the most prominent being Gilbert's *Palomar* stories and Jaime's *Hoppers 13* (aka *Locas*) stories. It also contains one-offs, shorter stories, surrealist jokes, and more.

Palomar tells the story of a fictional village in Latin America and its inhabitants. Its vibrant characters and sometimes-fantastic events are sometimes compared to the magical realism literary style of authors such as Gabriel García Márquez. The series is also sometimes referred to as *Heartbreak Soup*, after the first story set in Palomar.

Gilbert and Jaime Hernandez at the 2007 ComicCon. Gilbert is in the middle, Jaime is in the green shirt.

Hoppers 13 follows the tangled lives of a group of primarily chicano characters, from their teenage years in the early days of the California punk scene to the present day. (Hoppers, or Huerta, is a fictional city based on the Hernandezes' home town of Oxnard, California.) Two memorable members of Jaime's cast are Margarita Luisa "Maggie" Chascarrillo and Esperanza "Hopey" Leticia Glass, whose on-again, off-again romance is a focus for many *Hoppers 13* storylines. The series is also often called *Locas* (Spanish for "crazy women") because of the many quirky female characters depicted.

One aspect of the *Love and Rockets* opus is the way Los Bros Hernandez portray the passage of time in a relatively realistic manner despite the traditional constraints of the medium. For example, Maggie's character, a pro-solar mechanic, debuted as a slight yet curvy young adult living in a world both distinctly chicano and punk with a sci-fi twist. As Jaime developed her character in more detail, she started to gain weight slowly. Over the years, Maggie and the other characters have evolved, growing more layered and complex as their stories develop. The present Maggie is now the manager of an apartment complex with bleached blonde hair and a penchant for wearing sexy bathing suits on her rubenesque figure. Jaime has also made extensive use of flashbacks, with Maggie and the others presented at different ages from toddlers through teenagers and young adults to thirtysomethings. The first issue of volume two of *Love and Rockets* featured a cover with a range of different Maggie ages/looks.

The original runs of *Palomar* and *Locas* have each been collected in recent one-volume editions by Fantagraphics (see Palomar (graphic novel)), although not all of the stories involving "Locas" and "Palomar" characters are contained in these collections. The original fifty-issue Love and Rockets "Volume One" has also been reprinted in its entirety in both a fifteen-volume paperback library, and more recently a seven-volume mass-market paperback series by Fantagraphics. In addition, several hardcovers collect edited versions of the series tales.

Many attempts have been made to make L&R into a movie, or series of movies. However, until recently, the movie rights had been held up in litigation for over 15 years.

Characters

Jaime

Love and Rockets #31 by Gilbert and Jaime Hernandez, 1989, Fantagraphics Books.
Cover illustration by Jamie Hernandez depicting his two main characters, Maggie (right) and Hopey.

- **Margarita Luisa "Maggie" Chascarrillo:** best friend (and occasional lover) of Hopey; otherwise dates men, most prominently Ray Dominguez. Befriended Hopey in the punk rock scene of their southern Californian home town. Briefly becomes a world-travelling Pro-solar mechanic who goes on science-fiction flavored adventures in the early issues. Maggie along with Hopey were ranked #95 on Wizard Magazine's 200 Greatest Comic Book Characters of all time.
- **Esperanza Leticia "Hopey" Glass:** sharp-tongued, wild and adventurous best friend of Maggie. Portrayed usually as a lesbian. Plays bass very poorly in a series of punk bands.
- **Beatríz "Penny Century" García:** bombshell friend to Maggie/Hopey and wife of the ridiculously wealthy H.R. Costigan.
- **Isabel "Izzy" Reubens:** Friend/mentor to Maggie. A writer who suffers a nervous breakdown after a divorce/abortion, becoming a notorious "witch lady" in Maggie's hometown.
- **Daphne "Daffy" Matsumoto:** a rich young friend of Maggie and Hopey who is a prominent supporting character in the early comics, but later goes off to college.
- **Ray Dominguez:** one of Maggie's boyfriends, a painter. Jaime follows his life from Hoppers to LA.
- **Doyle Blackburn:** Ray's childhood friend, who struggles with a history of violence.
- **Rena Titañon and Vicki Glori:** stars of the Mexican women wrestling world. Rena is Maggie's friend. Rival Vicki is Maggie's aunt.
- **Danita Lincoln:** Maggie's coworker at Vandy's. She dates Ray after Maggie leaves town; also works as a stripper with Doyle's girlfriend Lily.
- **H.R. Costigan:** horned billionaire who has on-again, off-again affair with Penny Century.
- **Terry Downe:** talented, coldly pretty guitar player who still pines for ex-girlfriend Hopey.
- **Rand Race:** handsome, world-famous pro-solar mechanic who hires Maggie and takes her on adventures, oblivious to her crush on him.
- **Eulalio "Speedy" Ortiz:** Isabel's brother, a member of the local "Hoppers" gang, shared a mutual crush on Maggie until his untimely death.
- **Vivian "Frogmouth" Solis:** a troublemaking stripper and aspiring actress that Ray first develops a crush on and then begrudgingly becomes friends with. Separately, she is friends with Maggie.

Gilbert

- **Luba:** hammer-wielding, sexually promiscuous, enormously busty, no-nonsense mayor of Palomar.
- **Luba's children:** Maricela, Guadalupe, Doralis, Casimira, Socorro, Joselito, Concepcion.
- **Luba's lovers:** Archie, Khamo, Peter, Jose.
- **Ofelia:** Luba's cousin who helped raise her and her children.
- **Heraclio and Carmen:** a loving couple who served as central characters for many early Palomar stories.
- **Israel, Satch, Vincete, Jesús:** Heraclio and Pipo's childhood gang of friends.
- **Chelo:** sheriff of Palomar, midwife who delivered many of the main characters.
- **Pipo, Gato, Sergio:** beautiful, vain Pipo; her angry but devoted husband Gato, and her son (by Manuel) Sergio. a world-famous soccer star.
- **Tonantzín:** beautiful, hard-partying Palomar girl who becomes passionately politically active.
- **Manuel and Soledad:** friends/lovers/rivals, stars of the first Palomar story "Heartbreak Soup"
- **Fritz, Petra, Venus:** Fritz and Petra are Luba's long-lost half-sisters who share her voluptuous figure and penchant for adventure. Venus is Petra's precocious, comics-loving daughter.
- **María:** Luba's mother, who abandoned her when she was a toddler. Emigrated to United States and became mother to Fritz and Petra.
- **Errata Stigmata:** a somewhat surreal character who develops stigmata as a reaction to severe emotional trauma. Her first appearance was in "Radio Zero" and her origin is told in "Tears from Heaven".

Landmark stories

This list provides an example of the types of stories that helped *Love and Rockets* gain critical acclaim.

Jaime

- Mechanics - the original "Maggie the mechanic" story, in which Maggie travels to Africa with a group of Pro-solar mechanics and becomes caught in the middle of a political revolution. Introduced Jaime's striking artwork and confident storytelling style.
- The Death of Speedy Ortiz- Jaime moves away from the "Maggie the mechanic" stories to permanently settle on adventures in Maggie's

personal life. Maggie's longtime crush Speedy commits suicide. She also begins dating the understated artist Ray.
- Flies on the Ceiling - The story of Isabel Reuben's nervous breakdown in Mexico, where she moves after having an abortion and a divorce.
- Wigwam Bam - Hopey leaves Maggie and her hometown of Hoppers to find adventures, dealing with being too old for her punk rock lifestyle.
- Home School - Using Peanuts and Dennis the Menace inspired artwork, Jaime tells the story of toddler Maggie and slightly-older Isabel becoming friends under the shadow of fighting parents.
- The Ghost of Hoppers - Grown-up Maggie, now an apartment manager in the San Fernando valley, sees visions of ghosts after a creepy visit from Isabel (*from* Love and Rockets Vol. 2).

Gilbert

- Heartbreak Soup - First Palomar story. Tells the story of notorious ladies' man Manuel, and his affair with beautiful 14-year-old Pipo, and its effect on his friendship with repressed misanthrope Soledad.
- An American in Palomar - A self-important American photographer tries to frame Palomar as a downtrodden, poverty-stricken town to further his own career.
- For the Love of Carmen - A one-issue meditation on the marriage of Heraclio and Carmen Calderon, citizens of Palomar.
- Human Diastrophism - Palomar's residents hunt for a serial killer as Luba finds herself helplessly in love with a young construction worker, and hard-partying Tonantzin becomes politically active. Published in book form under the title Blood of Palomar.
- Love and Rockets X - Mostly set outside of Palomar, a young, white garage band named Love and Rockets runs into racism between blacks and whites; as well as clashes between rich and poor through Los Angeles. Set near the time of the 1992 riots. Tangentially inspired by how the actual English band Love and Rockets got their name from this comics series.
- Poison River - An immensely complex story of Luba's pre-Palomar life. Details a complex plot involving the Mexican government, the mob, transsexuals, racist comic books and Luba's beauty queen mother Maria.

Graphic novels and collections

All published at Fantagraphics :
1. **Music for Mechanics**, by Los Bros Hernandez*, October 1985, ~140 pages
(* principally Gilbert & Jaime Hernandez; some pages by Mario) Preface by Carter Scholz
2. **Chelo's Burden**, by Los Bros Hernandez, June 1986, ~150 pages Preface by Gary Groth
3. **Las Mujeres Perdidas**, by Los Bros Hernandez (only Gilbert and Jaime), August 1987, ~140 pages
4. **Tears from Heaven**, by Los Bros Hernandez (Gilbert and Jaime; one cover reproduction by Mario), January 1988, ~125 pages
5. **House of Raging Women**, by Los Bros Hernandez (only Gilbert and Jaime from now on), September 1988, ~125 pages
6. **Duck Feet**, by Los Bros Hernandez, September 1988, ~125 pages
7. **The Death of Speedy**, by Jaime Hernandez, November 1989, ~125 pages
8. **Blood of Palomar**, by Gilbert Hernandez, December 1989, ~125 pages
9. **Flies on the Ceiling**, by Los Bros Hernandez (principally Jaime), October 1991, ~110 pages
10. **X**, by Gilbert Hernandez, July 1993, ~90 pages
11. **Wigwam Bam**, by Jaime Hernandez, March 1994, ~125 pages
12. **Poison River**, by Gilbert Hernandez, September 1994, ~190 pages
13. **Chester Square**, by Jaime Hernandez, July 1996, ~155 pages
14. **Luba Conquers the World**, by Gilbert Hernandez, December 1996, ~130 pages
15. **Hernandez Satyricon**, by Los Bros Hernandez (Mario, Gilbert & Jaime Hernandez), August 1997, ~110 pages
16. **Whoa Nellie!**, by Jaime Hernandez, June 2000, ~70 pages
17. **Fear of Comics**, by Gilbert Hernandez, October 2000, ~120 pages
18. **Locas in Love**, by Jaime Hernandez, October 2000, ~120 pages (End of Volume 1)
19. **Luba in America** ("Luba", Tome 1), by Gilbert Hernandez, 2001, ~165 pages (Starts with Volume 2)
20. **Dicks and Deedees**, by Jaime Hernandez, June 2003, ~90 pages
21. **The Book of Ofelia** ("Luba", Tome 2), by Gilbert Hernandez, December 2005, ~250 pages
22. **Ghost of Hoppers**, by Jaime Hernandez, December 2005, ~120 pages
23. **Three Daughters** ("Luba", Tome 3), by Gilbert Hernandez, August 2006, ~140 pages
24. **The Education of Hopey Glass**, by Jaime Hernandez, April 2008, ~130 pages (End of Volume 2)
25. **High Soft Lisp**, by Gilbert Hernandez, April 2010, ~140 pages

Re-releases

Volume 1 was re-released in smaller "omnibus" style trade paperbacks. Starting in 2010, volume 2's stories began getting re-releases as well.
1. *Maggie the Mechanic*, by Jamie Hernandez (Locas Book 1, from Volume I) -272 pages
2. *The Girl from H.O.P.P.E.R.S.*, by Jamie Hernandez (Locas Book 2, from Volume I) -272 pages
3. *Perla la Loca*, by Jamie Hernandez (Locas Book 3, from Volume I) -288 pages
4. *Heartbreak Soup*, by Gilbert Hernandez (Palomar Book 1, from Volume I) -288 pages
5. *Human Diastrophism*, by Gilbert Hernandez (Palomar Book 2, from Volume I) -288 pages
6. *Beyond Palomar*, by Gilbert

Hernandez (Palomar Book 3, from Volume I) -256 pages
7. *Amor Y Cohetes*, by Jamie & Gilbert Hernandez (Non-Loca and Palomar comics from Volume I) -280 pages
8. *Penny Century*, by Jamie Hernandez (Locas Book 4, from "Penny Century" and "Whoa, Nellie!" comics, plus "Maggie and Hopey Color Fun") -240 pages

Hardcovers
Edited segments of both the Palomar and the Maggie stories are available in hardcover format.
1. Locas: The Maggie and Hopey Stories
2. Locas II: Maggie, Hopey, and Ray
3. Palomar: The Heartbreak Soup Stories
4. Luba

New stories
The series continues in annual trade paperbacks, entitled *Love & Rockets: New Stories*. To date, three exist:
1. *New Stories*, volume 1, 112 pages (2008)
2. *New Stories*, volume 2, 104 pages (2009)
3. *New Stories*, volume 3, 104 pages (2010)

Source (edited): "http://en.wikipedia.org/wiki/Love_and_Rockets_(comics)"

Nothing Nice to Say

Nothing Nice to Say is a webcomic, touted as "The world's FIRST online punk comic", created by artist **Mitch Clem**. It is sometimes abbreviated as *Nothing Nice*, *NNTS* or *NN2S*.

Synopsis
First launched online in February, 2002, *Nothing Nice To Say* follows roommates Blake and Fletcher, while living in Minneapolis, Minnesota, as they make fun of punk rock, punk rock fans, and just about everything relating to the punk subculture, including themselves. Although it follows the de facto 3-panel webcomic setup of two roommates with one being slightly off-the-wall, it is unique in placing them in a punk setting.

History
During much of the comic's existence, Mitch used the space under the comic as his blog. Now his blog can be found at his LiveJournal (See Link Below).

Clem's blogs began to show that he was likely suffering bouts of depression. Because of this he was mocked on the comic's own discussion forum; the internet traffic for which had rapidly outgrown the traffic for the comic strip. This is allegedly one of the reasons that Mitch- somewhat unceremoniously - ended the comic in 2004. At this time, Mitch told fans he would be collaborating on a strip called *Joe and Monkey* with fellow webcomic artist Zach Miller.

Clem left Joe and Monkey before the series even launched, but did return to take over writing and illustration duties for the entire month of January 2005, at which point Mitch announced he would resurrect *Nothing Nice* in what would become the now familiar black and white format, as opposed to the original run, which was in color.

Updates slowed sometime after January 2006, when Clem began focusing his energy on a new autobiographical strip called *San Antonio Rock City*. Eventually, *Nothing Nice* was put on indefinite hiatus and *SARC* became Clem's main focus.

Mitch Clem stated that he was unopposed to bringing back *Nothing Nice* (though perhaps at a less frequent schedule), and stayed true to this statement when he brought it back on a weekly schedule on August 28, 2006. Updates ranged from sporadic to nonexistent for a while as the focus shifted from *SARC* to *NN2S* and back. Clem eventually quit *San Antonio Rock City* after breaking up with his then-girlfriend who served as the series' co-star, and turned his focus back to *Nothing Nice*, where it continued to update on a mostly regular thrice weekly schedule. *Nothing Nice* went back on temporary hiatus as Clem began work on another autobiographical strip, *My Stupid Life*. Nothing Nice to Say resumed on September 15, 2008. NN2S has been on hiatus since December 23, 2008.

Main cast
Blake

Blake and Fletcher as they appeared in the early strips

One of the comic's main characters. He is named after Blake Schwarzenbach of Jawbreaker and Jets to Brazil fame (also has an obvious resemblance to Jawbreaker-era Schwarzenbach), and is a great fan of both bands. Tends to be the voice of reason of the two main characters. Besides Schwarzenbach bands, he is also a fan of pop-punk bands and even some indie rock bands. Played guitar in a band with Fletcher, called *The Negative Adjectives*. He has a shrine to Henry Rollins in his bedroom, something Fletcher was unaware of until September 13, 2006. Blake is considered by many fans to represent a sort of "parallel universe Mitch", or is at least modelled on the comic's author; the parallels between certain of their life events and their shared tastes and opinions are used as evidence for this.

Fletcher
Blake's bald-headed roommate. Did not originally have a name; instead he was named through a reader contest. Tends to come up with some fairly crazy and somewhat anti-social ideas, sometimes resulting in litigation. He is also sometimes attracted to irritating behaviors and habits simply for their ability to anger others, such as his taking up smoking. Often wears a band shirt that reads "BAND". Is a fan of 1980s hardcore punk. Played drums for *The Negative Adjectives*. Recently contracted a case of "pop punk" at a show. He is often a comic foil to Blake's role as straightman and the two most often provide the main thrust of the series' plotlines.

Phillip
Originally a ska fan, he now listens to emo and vehemently denies having ever liked ska at all; this is plotted by the author to make fun of what he perceives to be the trend-hopping nature of most modern-day emo fans. Blames the female gender for most of his problems, even though they actually tend to be self-inflicted. Also seems to exude "whiny bitch pheromones" which make it impossible to stay around him for any longer time without resorting to physical violence. He started out 2007 by renouncing emo in favor of what he felt was less depressing pop-punk, but after buying the newest pop punk album (implied to be the album "Hospitals" by Off With Their Heads), he hanged himself in his apartment. His name is an obvious tongue-in-cheek reference to the comedian Emo Phillips.

Cecil
An anthropomorphic gopher (refential to the strip's setting of the Twin Cities of Minnesota.) Very sarcastic, and at one time insulted people for spare change. According to the comic, has played bass for Screeching Weasel, roadied for Fifteen and secretly written songs for The Donnas. Played bass for *The Negative Adjectives* before he quit right before their first show. Cecil has apparently rejoined the band since Joe Banks (see below) joined. Usually seen wearing a Quincy Punx shirt.

Charlie/Chris
A vegan, hardcore-crust punk. The rest of the cast tends to walk on egg shells around him due to his veganism, as they're afraid they might upset him if he so much as touches an object that has been in contact with dairy products. He has been referred to as both "Charlie" and "Chris," an error that Clem has jokingly acknowledged.

Karen
A radical feminist (riot grrl). Spends a lot of her time getting upset at Blake and Fletcher for allegedly objectifying female punk rock band members, yet started dating Alice only because a "strong lesbian stance" would improve her image as a feminist.

Joe
The comic's youngest character. He's a skater and tends to get made fun of by Blake and Fletcher, as they see most skaters as "corporate whores". He confused buttons of fashion companies with wearing "cool" buttons of punk bands.

Joe Banks
In 2005, Nothing Nice To Say and Joe and Monkey had a crossover, featuring Joe, the titular hero of the latter, auditioning for Blake and Fletcher's band, The Negative Adjectives (after seeing a poster written by Fletcher proclaiming that the band needed no new members). Ironically, Banks was accepted as the band's new singer and second guitarist and has since been featured in strips featuring the band performing.

Other recurring characters

Skar
A skinhead oi! punk, and is mistaken by Blake and Fletcher for a Nazi.

Alice
A goth girl and a lesbian, dating Karen.

Bort
Was originally straight edge, but has since broke his edge and started drinking as well as smoking. Has straight edge X's tattooed on the back of his hands, and is prone to violence when one points out the irony in having them and consuming alcohol and tobacco.

The Hippie Chick
Also known as *That Hippie Chick Who Works At The Coffee Shop* is hinted at having dated Alice. Not much else is known about her, other than that she is in fact a hippie and likes the Grateful Dead and Phish.

The Ska Dude
Doesn't have a name. Was introduced because Mitch wanted a ska dude.

Cthulhu
Originally from the H. P. Lovecraft stories. He's lived in Blake and Fletcher's closet for, presumably, the entire series, though he has only shown up a couple of times. Most recently, Cthulhu was turned into a kitten, though his subsequent trip to the sewers, where he raised a C.H.U.D. to eat the person who turned him into a kitten, suggests he still has his powers.

Zach Miller
Has appeared in some NN2S comics. Creator of Joe and Monkey and the late No Pants Tuesday.

Mitch Clem
Mitch often appears in his own comics, often arguing with Blake & Fletcher via intercom, and was once sighted drawing the comic at a coffee shop.

Spin-offs and related content

San Antonio Rock City
San Antonio Rock City, or SARC, was an autobiographical webcomic about Mitch and his weekly exploits with then-girlfriend Victoria. This comic was updated consistently several times each week, eventually going daily, for approx 6 months, and featured several references to Nothing Nice, including a strip with cameos of Blake, Fletcher, Cecil, Joe Banks, and the Anarchist Fan. Mitch quit the series permanently after he and Victoria broke up in early 2007.

The Coffee Achievers

The Coffee Achievers originally started out as Nothing Nice story arc, but later turned into its own comic as a collaboration with Joe Dunn, from Joe Loves Crappy Movies. The cast is mostly the same as that of Nothing Nice, but with small alterations, and is not considered to take place in the same universe as Nothing Nice To Say.

The Coffee Achievers began a working relationship between Clem and Joe Dunn that has now developed into a partnership, with Dunn serving as Clem's go-to colorist for his prolific work creating concert fliers and album art. The two have also expressed plans to eventually team up again for Clem's long-planned post-apocalyptic saga **"The Rain Dogs"**.

Source (edited): "http://en.wikipedia.org/wiki/Nothing_Nice_to_Say"

Peter Pank

Peter Pank is a Spanish comic book written and drawn by *Max*, the pseudonym of Francesc Capdevila.

Peter Pank is an adult-oriented parody of J.M. Barrie's *Peter Pan*. While in the original, Peter is simply a boy who refused to grow up to a man, in *Peter Pank* he's a vicious, rebellious, belligerent punk with a "No Future" attitude.

The comic mostly follows a parodied version of *Peter and Wendy*'s plot, but is heavily influenced by punk culture and anarchism. Various characters have been replaced with more "adult" versions: the Lost Boys are punks, the Indians are hippies, the pirates are rockers, and the mermaids are BDSM dominas. Many parts of the comic have a pornographic style, including both male and female nudity.

The comic ends with Peter sentenced to be hanged for rape and Wendy and her brothers returning home, Wendy having become a prostitute and her brothers drug addicts.

Source (edited): "http://en.wikipedia.org/wiki/Peter_Pank"

Tank Girl

cover art to *Tank Girl: The Odyssey*

Tank Girl is a British comic created by Jamie Hewlett and Alan Martin. Originally drawn by Jamie Hewlett, the strip has recently been drawn by Rufus Dayglo, Ashley Wood, and Mike McMahon.

The eponymous character Tank Girl drives a tank, which is also her home. She undertakes a series of missions for a nebulous organization before making a serious mistake and being declared an outlaw for her sexual inclinations and her substance abuse. The comic centres on her misadventures with her boyfriend, Booga, a mutant kangaroo. The comic's style was heavily influenced by punk visual art, and strips were frequently deeply disorganized, anarchic, absurdist, and psychedelic. The strip features various elements with origins in surrealist techniques, fanzines, collage, cut-up technique, stream of consciousness, and metafiction, with very little regard or interest for conventional plot or committed narrative.

The strip was initially set in a stylized post-apocalyptic Australia, although it drew heavily from contemporary British pop culture.

Publication history

Martin and Hewlett first met in the mid-1980s in Worthing, when Martin was in a band with Philip Bond called the University Smalls. One of their tracks was a song called "Rocket Girl". They had started adding the suffix 'girl' to everything habitually after the release of the *Supergirl* movie, but "Rocket Girl" was a student at college who Bond had a crush on and apparently bore a striking resemblance to a *Love and Rockets* character. They began collaborating on a comic/fanzine called *Atomtan*, and while working on this, Jamie had drawn

" a grotty looking beefer of a girl brandishing an unfeasible firearm. One of our friends was working on a project to design a pair of headphones and was basing his design on the type used by World War II tank driver. His studio in Worthing was littered with loads of photocopies of combat vehicles. Alan pinched one of the images and gave it to Jamie who then stuck it behind his grotty girl illustrations and then added a logo which read 'Tank Girl'. "

The image was published in the fanzine as a one-page ad (with a caption that read: "SHE'LL BREAK YOUR BACK AND YOUR BALLS!"), but the *Tank Girl* series first appeared in the debut issue of *Deadline* (1988), a UK magazine intended as a forum for new comic talent, or as its publishers Brett Ewins and Tom Astor put it, "a forum for the wild, wacky and hitherto unpublishable," and it continued until the end of the magazine in 1995.

Tank Girl became quite popular in the politicized indie counterculture zeitgeist as a cartoon mirror of the growing empowerment of women in punk rock culture. Posters and t-shirts began springing up everywhere, including one especially made for the Clause 28 march against Margaret Thatcher's legislation. Clause 28 stated that a local authority "shall not intentionally promote homosexuality or publish material with the intention of promoting homosexuality" or "promote the teaching in any maintained school of the acceptability of homosexuality as a pretended family relationship." Deadline publisher Tom Astor said, "In London, there are even weekly lesbian gatherings called 'Tank Girl nights.'"

With public interest growing, Penguin, the largest publishing company in Britain, bought the rights to collect the strips as a book, and before long, Tank Girl had been published in Spain, Italy, Germany, Scandinavia, Argentina, Brazil and Japan, with several US publishers fighting over the license. Finally Dark Horse Comics won out, and the strips were reprinted in color beginning in '91, with an extended break in '92, and ending in September '93. A graphic novel-length story named Tank Girl: The Odyssey was also published in '95, written by Peter Milligan and loosely inspired by Homer's Odyssey, Joyce's Ulysses and a considerable quantity of junk TV, (although Milligan asserts in the preface that the story is entirely based on real events, inspired by the wanderings and adventures of a group of lost friends, all of whom appear in the pages under various pseudonyms). Another graphic novel called Tank Girl: Apocalypse, in which TG becomes pregnant, also appeared in '96, written by Alan Grant after he spent several hours alone in the pitch-dark bowels of an actual tank, experiencing sensory deprivation. Apocalypse was drawn by Philip Bond. These last two stories, being graphic novels and not compilations of the strips, are distinctly more linear in nature, Apocalypse having absolutely no involvement from either Martin or Hewlett (and being dramatically less well-received by fans).

Characters

- **Tank Girl**. Her real name in the strip is Rebecca Buck, but this is very rarely mentioned throughout. According to her own history included as a preface to one of the books, her first words were "cauliflower penis". When she was 7, she started a collection of novelty pencil sharpeners (the collection is now housed in the National Museum of Modern Pencil Sharpeners, Sydney). She later became a tank pilot and worked as a bounty hunter before shooting a heavily decorated officer, having mistaken him for her father, and failing to deliver colostomy bags to President Hogan, the incontinent Head of State in Australia, resulting in him publicly embarrassing himself at a large international trade conference. These events resulted in Tank Girl becoming an outlaw with a multi-million dollar bounty on her head. She is prone to random acts of sex and violence, hair dyeing, flatulence, nose-picking, vomiting, spitting, and more than occasional drunkenness. She also has the ability to outrun any ice-cream van.
- **Booga**: a mutated kangaroo, formerly quite a successful toy designer of "products Santa would've sacrificed a reindeer for," and presently Tank Girl's devoted boyfriend. She met him when he sneaked into her tank one night to pinch a pair of her knickers. He is a big Dame Edna fan and once impersonated Bill Clinton. Booga, often against his will, always does the cooking, particularly the great British institution of tea. He follows TG everywhere and does, by his own admission, whatever she tells him. This includes murder.
- The talking stuffed animals:
- **Camp Koala**: a stitchy, brown, gay, koala-shaped stuffed toy described as "the Jeremy Thorpe of comics", whom TG sodomizes with a hot banana. Camp Koala died tragically when they were playing baseball with live hand grenades which Camp eagerly caught in the outfield, exploding on impact, resulting in a violent, bloody, and gruesome death. After a tearful and comical funeral service, the other characters go to a toy store and buy a new one. Campa Koala is known for visiting occasionally as a guardian angel. He is the only character TG's ever admitted to loving.
- **Squeaky toy rat**: a squeaky toy rat.
- **Mr. Precocious**: a "small Shakespearean mutant" who looks a bit like a mini bipedal pink elephant, though may possibly be a bilby.
- **Stevie**, a wild-haired blond Aborigine who owns a convenience store and chain-smokes. Being TG's ex-boyfriend, Booga is always a bit jealous of him. He has various familial ties and connections with Aboriginal culture and remote traditionalist tribespeople.
- **Barney**: busted out of a mental hospital by TG, she is more or less insane. In The Odyssey, she is responsible for killing the whole cast, thereby sending them all to the land of the dead, from which TG was forced to save them by finding the Prince of Farts.
- **Sub Girl** (real name unknown, although a trading card for the film once listed her real name as 'Subrina'). Described as "like a beautiful flower floating in the loo", she pilots a submarine. A friend of TG's since childhood, she used to come round her house with Jet Girl and try on her mum's underwear.
- **Jet Girl** (real name unknown), a talented mechanic who flies a jet. All her friends call her "boring" (she has admitted to being a big fan of Rod Stewart).
- **Boat Girl**. Otherwise known as Jackie. Barney's nervous hairdresser,

former figure skater. Her only brother killed by TG and Booga after they stole from a church. She owns a greatly modified WWII Motor Torpedo Boat.

The future of *Tank Girl*

After the 1995 film, Hewlett went on to make his fortune creating Gorillaz with Blur's Damon Albarn. Gorillaz were a virtual band for which Hewlett reportedly received a "big money" offer from Dreamworks for the film rights. Hewlett declined, still soured from his previous Hollywood experience, and opted to wait until he could control things on the project himself.

Martin wandered around for a bit, staying at communes with hippie friends, looking for stone circles and ancient sites before settling in Berwick Upon Tweed in the Scottish Borders with his wife Lou and son Rufus Bodie (named after Lewis Collins' character in *The Professionals*). Martin has played in various bands, written a Tank Girl "novel" (*Armadillo*) published in March 2008 by Titan Books, as well as various screenplays and scripts. He wrote the first new Tank Girl limited series in over ten years: *Tank Girl: The Gifting* with award-winning Australian artist Ashley Wood and Rufus Dayglo. Published by American publishers IDW, the first issue of which was released in June 2007. He is also producing *Tank Girl: Carioca* with Brit comics' legend Mike McMahon for Titan Books which should see print in September 2011.

" We went to the comics graveyard and dug her up. She's smelling pretty bad, but we're gonna put her in a wheelbarrow and parade her around for all to see, anyway. "

Summer 2008 saw *Tank Girl: Skidmarks* appearing in all-new Nine-page episodes in the *Judge Dredd Megazine*, again written by Martin, with art duties taken on by Rufus Dayglo, who drew *Visions of Booga* for IDW Comics. In an interview Martin revealed that *Visions of Booga* was the only Tank Girl comic that doesn't contain any major swear words: "It has a "bastard" here and a "bitch" there, but it doesn't have any F-words or C-words."

Titan Books have released *The Cream of Tank Girl*, compiled by Alan Martin, containing Jamie Hewlett art and Alan Martin scripts, starting from her earliest beginning as a pin-up in *Atomtan*, it features a brand new Hewlett cover as well as brand new script from Martin.

Comic books

Tank Girl - By Hewlett & Martin. Released in 1990 by Penguin Books, collected the first 18 episodes from Deadline Magazine.

Tank Girl 2 - By Hewlett & Martin. Released in 1993 by Penguin Books, collected 20 episodes of the Tank Girl story.

Tank Girl 3 by Hewlett & Martin was published by Penguin in 1996. It collected the final stories from Deadline Magazine.

- Tank Girl 1, Tank Girl 2, and Tank Girl 3 were subsequently reprinted by Titan Books and the stories were rearranged into correct chronological order for the recent Tank Girl Remastered series, again by Titan Books.

When the Tank Girl movie was being made, a deal was struck with DC's imprint Vertigo Comics to release three Tank Girl mini-series. The first two were released throughout June 1995 - February 1996. The third mini-series was never created.

- **Tank Girl: The Odyssey** was a four issue mini-series published by Vertigo Comics June 1995 - October 1995. Titan Books collected this mini-series in July 2003, with a 'Remastered' trade released in November 2009.
- **Tank Girl: Apocalypse** was a four issue mini-series published by Vertigo Comics in November 1995 - February 1996. Titan Books collected this mini-series in October 2003, with a 'Remastered' trade released in February 2010.

In 2007, Tank Girl returned with new mini-series and one-shots.

- **Tank Girl: The Gifting** was a four issue mini-series by Wood, Dayglo & Martin, published by IDW from May 2007 - August 2007. These four issues were collected in trade paperback format in November 2007.
- **Tank Girl: Visions of Booga** was a four issue mini-series Dayglo & Martin, published by IDW from May 2008 - August 2008. These four issues were collected in trade paperback format in November 2008.
- **Tank Girl: Skidmarks** was a four issue mini-series by Dayglo & Martin, published by Titan Comics from November 2009 - February 2010. The trade paperback collection of these four issues is scheduled to be released in July 2010.
- **Tank Girl: Dark Nuggets** was a one-shot issue by Dayglo & Martin, published by Image Comics in January 2010. It was the first of a series of three Tank Girl one-shots published by Image Comics. The three issues will be collected with bonus material in the trade paperback We Hate Tank Girl, due for release 4 December 2010.
- **Tank Girl: Dirty Helmets** was the second Dayglo & Martin one-shot published by Image Comics. It was released in April 2010.
- **Tank Girl: The Royal Escape** is a four issue mini-series by Dayglo & Martin, published by IDW from March 2010 - June 2010. A trade paperback collection was released in September 2010, with a UK edition to follow.
- **Tank Girl: Hairy Heroes** was the third one-shot published by Image Comics, in August 2010.
- **Tank Girl: Bad Wind Rising** is a four issue mini-series by Dayglo & Martin. The first issue was released by Titan Comics in November 2010.
- **Tank Girl: Carioca** is a six part mini-series drawn by Mick McMahon and written by Alan Martin that is scheduled to be

released September 2011. Tank Girl has been collected into a number of trade paperbacks over the years. The entire back catalogue was reprinted by Titan books in 2002 and these books were "re-mastered" in anniversary editions, stripped of their subsequently-added computer colouring and line work repaired.

- *Tank Girl Book 1* consists of the first 15 episodes, originally published in Deadline Magazine, starting Sept. '88, all originally in black and white.
- *Tank Girl Book 2* consists of the next 17 episodes, some colour, some black and white.
- *Tank Girl Book 3* rounds up a final 9 episodes, including some featuring Booga as the star. All in colour.
- *Tank Girl - The Odyssey* consists of 4 issues released between June and October 1995, published by DC's Vertigo imprint. These comics were printed in full colour.
- *Tank Girl - Apocalypse* consists of 4 issues released between November 1995 and February 1996, published by DC's Vertigo imprint. Again these comics were in full colour.
- A graphic novel adaptation of the movie was also released by Penguin books in 1995.
- *Tank Girl: The Gifting* trade paperback (four issue mini-series published by IDW Publishing) was released in November 2007.
- *Tank Girl: Armadillo and a Bushel of Other Stories* (Novel, Fiction, text by Alan Martin, cover art by Jamie Hewlett) released by Titan Books in March 2008.
- *Tank Girl: Visions of Booga* trade paperback (four issue mini-series published by IDW Publishing) was released in May 2008.
- *Tank Girl: SkidMarks* trade paperback (12 part series in the Judge Dredd Megazine, published in the US by Titan Books as a four issue mini-series) released in July 2010.
- "Tank Girl: The Royal Escape" trade paperback (four issue mini-series published by IDW publishing) was released in September 2010.
- "We Hate Tank Girl" trade paperback (Collects the Tank Girl One-Shots: Dark Nuggets, Dirty Helmets, and Hairy Heroes) was released February 2011.

Film

The comic was also adapted into a critically and financially unsuccessful film, albeit with a considerable cult following. The film featured Lori Petty as Tank Girl and Naomi Watts as Jet Girl.

Martin and Hewlett are known for speaking poorly of the experience, with Martin calling it "a bit of a sore point" for them. Despite its critics, the film did however undeniably broaden the comics' fanbase from a relatively modest cult following to an international audience.

Source (edited): "http://en.wikipedia.org/wiki/Tank_Girl"

The Invisibles

The Invisibles is a comic book series that was published by the Vertigo imprint of DC Comics from 1994 to 2000. It was created and scripted by Scottish writer Grant Morrison, and drawn by various artists throughout its publication.

The plot follows (more or less) a single cell of The Invisible College, a secret organization battling against physical and psychic oppression using time travel, magic, meditation, and physical violence.

For most of the series, the team includes leader King Mob; Lord Fanny, a Brazilian transsexual shaman; Boy, a former member of the NYPD; Ragged Robin, a telepath with a mysterious past; and Jack Frost, a young hooligan from Liverpool who may be the next Buddha. Their enemies are the Archons of Outer Church, interdimensional alien gods who have already enslaved most of the human race without its knowledge.

Publication history

The Invisibles was Morrison's first major creator-owned title for DC Comics and it drew from his *Zenith* strip as well as 1990s conspiracy culture. His intent was to create a *hypersigil* to jump-start the culture in a more positive direction.

The title initially sold well but sales dipped sharply during the first series, leading to concerns that the series might be canceled outright. To counteract this, Morrison suggested a "wankathon" in the hope of bringing about a magical increase in sales by a mass of fans simultaneously masturbating at a set time.

Morrison became seriously ill while writing the book, something he attributes to working on the title and the manner in which its magical influence affected him, and has stated that his work on the comic made him into a different person from the one who started it. He has also said that much of the story was told to him by aliens when he was abducted during a trip to Katmandu.

The third and final series was meant to be a countdown to the new millennium but shipping delays meant the final issue did not appear until April 2000. All of the series have been collected in a set of trade paperbacks.

Morrison saw the series censored due to the publisher's concern over the possibility of paedophilic and child abuse content. The first such case was in volume one, issue 7 ("Arcadia part 3 : 120 Days Of Sod All"); dialogue was altered in one scene where a group rapes and degrades several nameless characters, and the term *lost souls* was used to ensure the characters could not be identified as children, as in the Marquis De Sade's original *120 Days of Sodom*, the book the characters find themselves trapped in. Later in the series the names of people and organizations were simply blacked out, much to Morrison's dismay. DC had one line that originally read "Walt Disney was a shit" blacked out at the suggestions of their lawyers; many of these examples of censorship were restored when reprinted in trade paperback.

The title was optioned to be made into a television series by BBC Scotland, but neither this nor an optioned film version have been made. Morrison wrote *The Filth* for Vertigo in 2002, which he describes as a companion piece to *The Invisibles*, though there is no other connection between the two titles.

Plot summary

Volume 1

Say You Want a Revolution

The first volume of *The Invisibles* introduces Dane McGowan, an angry teen from Liverpool, as he attempts to burn down his school. Abandoned by his father and neglected by his mother, Dane takes out his anger and frustration through destruction. In the first issue of the series, Dane is recruited by the Invisibles, a ragtag band of freedom fighters led by King Mob, a charismatic, cold-blooded assassin. The next arc, "Down and Out in Heaven and Hell", shows Dane as he tries to survive on his own in London after being abandoned by the Invisibles. Dane is mentored by Tom O'Bedlam, an old homeless man who is secretly a member of the Invisibles. Tom shows Dane the magic in the everyday world and helps him realize that his anger prevents him from experiencing real emotions. While wandering with Tom, Dane has a partially remembered alien abduction experience and is transported into a different dimension. Eventually Dane returns to the Invisibles, taking the codename "Jack Frost." The next arc, "Arcadia", follows the Invisibles as they go back in time via astral projection to the French Revolution. Jack is almost killed by a demonic agent of the Outer Church, the Invisibles' chief enemy. As the volume closes, Jack declares that he is leaving the Invisibles.

Apocalipstick

The second volume continues with Jack Frost abandoning the Invisibles. The tragic past of Lord Fanny, a Brazilian transvestite and a member of King Mob's Invisibles cell, is revealed in a story arc titled "She-Man", which jumps back and forth through time. After an encounter with an agent of the Outer Church, both King Mob and Lord Fanny are captured. The volume closes with a look at Jack as he evades both the Invisibles and the Outer Church in London. Jack remembers his abduction experience from the previous volume, recalling that his alien captors told him that he is the messiah. Jack is approached by Sir Miles, a high-ranking member of the Outer Church, who tries to recruit him. Jack refuses and battles Sir Miles telepathically. After winning the psychic duel, Jack escapes again, this time to Liverpool. This volume also introduces Jim Crow, a Haitian Invisible and Voodoo practitioner, and the Moonchild, a monstrous being who will one day be crowned the next King of England. The twelfth issue of the series, "Best Man Fall", fleshes out the character of a soldier whom King Mob killed in the previous volume.

Entropy in the U.K.

Sir Miles' interrogates King Mob in an arc titled "Gideon Stargrave in Entropy in the U.K." Ragged Robin and Boy, the other members of King Mob's Invisibles cell, team up with Jim Crow to rescue their teammates. In the 20th issue of the series, Boy reflects on her past while taking a train to Liverpool to bring Jack back into the fold. In the following issue, "Liverpool", Jack returns to his mother's flat where he tells her everything that has happened to him since joining the Invisibles. He admits that he is scared of the responsibilities that he now has as humanity's savior and no longer knows what to do. Jack recalls that when he traveled to a different dimension with Tom O'Bedlam, a sentient satellite called Barbelith forced Jack to feel the collective suffering of humanity. Remembering this agony and realizing that he can put an end to it, Jack finally accepts his role and agrees to help save his friends. The next arc focuses on the regrouped Invisibles as they attempt to rescue King Mob and Lord Fanny. During the Invisibles' battle with the Outer Church, Jack is told that he will be responsible for destroying the world on December 22, 2012. Jack fully realizes the power at his disposal, defeating an extra-dimensional Archon of the Outer Church and healing King Mob of his injuries. Jack also heals Sir Miles, who had been severely hurt during the battle. The volume closes with a look at an Invisible named Mr. Six as he searches for traces of the Moonchild.

Volume 2

Bloody Hell in America

The second volume begins a year after the events in London. The arc "Black Science" follows the Invisibles embarking on a mission after taking a year off in America at the New York estate of wealthy Invisible Mason Lang. While Jack Frost, Boy, and Lord Fanny explore New York City, King Mob and Ragged Robin begin a sexual relationship. Jolly Roger, an Invisible and an old friend of King Mob's, asks them to help her steal an AIDS vaccine from Dulce Base. There, the Invisibles face off against Mr. Quimper and Colonel Friday, two psychic agents of the Outer Church. The Invisibles are victorious, though Quimper plants a tiny part of his psyche in Ragged Robin's subconscious.

Counting to None

The Invisibles travel to San Francisco where they meet Takashi, an employee of Mason Lang's who is working on a time machine. Ragged Robin reveals that she has been sent from the future using a working version of Takashi's time machine when King Mob takes her to the dimension that the Invisible College, the Invisibles' headquarters, inhabits. Meanwhile, Jack Frost and Lord Fanny obtain a powerful supernatural device called the "Hand of Glory" from a mysterious trio called the "Harlequinade." In an arc titled "Sensitive Criminal", King Mob travels back in time via astral projection to learn from past Invisibles how to operate the Hand of Glory. In the following arc, "American Death Camp", Boy steals the Hand of Glory and attempts to use it to rescue her brother, whom she believes is being held in a secret detention camp in Washington. In reality, Boy is actually being deprogrammed by a separate cell of Invisibles who discovered that she had been brainwashed by the Outer Church to deliver the Hand to them.

Kissing Mister Quimper

The team vacation in New Orleans. Boy and Jack Frost acknowledge their feelings for each other and begin a brief relationship. The Invisibles then go back to Dulce to steal a powerful substance called "Magic Mirror" from the Outer Church in an arc titled "Black Science 2." Aware of Quimper's presence within her consciousness, Ragged Robin is able to trap and defeat him with Lord Fanny's help. In the Dulce facility, Jack is taken into the Magic Mirror substance where he is shown the horrific dimension that the Outer Church hails from. After leaving Dulce, Ragged Robin prepares to return to the future. Using the Hand of Glory as an engine, Takashi's time machine can be used to return her to her time. After saying goodbye to King Mob, with whom she has fallen in love, Robin leaves the past behind. In the final issue of the volume, Boy leaves the Invisibles and King Mob destroys Mason Lang's mansion, telling him that it is possible for even the most rigid man to change.

Volume 3

The Invisible Kingdom

Picking up a year after the previous volume, the third and final volume of the series follows the Invisibles as they prepare to stop the Moonchild from being used as a host for Rex Mundi, the extra-dimensional ruler of the Outer Church. Many of the Invisibles have significantly changed in this volume. King Mob no longer uses guns or kills people and Jack Frost has fully accepted his role as humanity's savior. The Invisibles also no longer consider themselves at war with the Outer Church. Instead, they are on a mission to rescue humanity before the world ends. The arc "The Invisible Kingdom" portrays the final battle between the Invisibles and the Outer Church. Sir Miles is killed, as is Jolly Roger (her body is later seen in a mass grave), while Jack Frost single-handedly defeats Rex Mundi. He then travels once again into the Magic Mirror and learns that the dimensions that the Outer Church and the Invisible College inhabit are one and the same. Afterwards, King Mob retires and devotes the rest of his life to nonviolence. Jack Frost and Lord Fanny are left to start their own Invisibles cell. Years later, on December 22, 2012, the world is about to end, just as predicted. Ragged Robin returns and is finally reunited with King Mob. Jack Frost then breaks the fourth wall and addresses the reader, stating that, "Our sentence is up." At that moment, the world ends and humanity transforms into its next stage of existence, guided by Jack Frost.

Creators

While Grant Morrison wrote the entire series, *The Invisibles* never had a regular art team. It was intended that each story arc would be illustrated by a separate artist. The artists to work on each issue are:

- Volume 1
  - Issues #1-4, 22-24: Steve Yeowell
  - Issues #5-9, 13-15: Jill Thompson
  - Issue #10: Chris Weston
  - Issue #11: John Ridgway
  - Issue #12: Steve Parkhouse
  - Issue #16, 21: Paul Johnson
  - Issues #17-19: Phil Jimenez
  - Issue #20: Tommy Lee Edwards
  - Issue #25: Mark Buckingham
- Volume 2
  - Issues #1-13: Phil Jimenez (Issue #9 has Jimenez on layouts only, with the pencils handled by Chris Weston, credited as "Space Boy")
  - Issues #14-17, 19-22: Chris Weston
  - Issue #18: Ivan Reis
- Volume 3
  - Issues #12-9: Philip Bond, Warren Pleece
  - Issues #8-5: Sean Phillips
  - Issue #4: Steve Yeowell, Ashley Wood, Steve Parkhouse, Philip Bond, Jill Thompson, John Ridgway
  - Issue #3: Steve Yeowell, Rian Hughes, John Ridgway, Michael Lark, Jill Thompson, Chris Weston
  - Issue #2: Steve Yeowell, The Pander Brothers, John Ridgway, Cameron Stewart, Ashley Wood, Mark Buckingham, Dean Ormston, Grant Morrison
  - Issue #1: Frank Quitely

Issues #4-2 included artistic collaborators who did not illustrate Morrison's scripts precisely as written. The most notable examples were the three pages Ashley Wood drew in Vol. 3, #2 that were later redrawn by Cameron Stewart for *The Invisible Kingdom* trade paperback.

Collected editions

The Invisibles has been collected into seven trade paperbacks:
- *Say You Want a Revolution*, published 1999-06-01. Collects Volume 1, Issues #1-8 (ISBN 1-5638-9267-7)
- *Apocalipstick*, published 2001-04-01. Collects Volume 1, Issues #9-16 (ISBN 1-5638-9702-4)
- *Entropy in the UK*, published 2001-08-01. Collects Volume 1, Issues #17-25 (ISBN 1-5638-9728-8)
- *Bloody Hell in America*, published 1998-02-01. Collects Volume 2, Issues #1-4 (ISBN 1-5638-9444-0)
- *Counting to None*, published 1999-03-01. Collects Volume 2, Issues #5-13 (ISBN 1-56389-489-0)
- *Kissing Mister Quimper*, published 2000-02-01. Collects Volume 2, Issues #14-22 (ISBN 1-5638-9600-1)
- *The Invisible Kingdom*, published 2002-12-01. Collects Volume 3, Issues #1-12 (ISBN 1-4012-0019-2)

Source (edited): "http://en.wikipedia.

org/wiki/The_Invisibles"

DJ DB

DJ DB (also known as DB Burkeman) is a British jungle/drum and bass DJ who moved from London to New York in 1989. He was an early pioneer in rave culture in the U.S. Also, he was partly responsible for bringing drum and bass to America. He was the co-founder of Breakbeat Science recordings & store, the first record store in the United States to specialize in drum and bass.

Career

Arriving in New York in 1989 from London , where he was resident DJ and promoter at the London version of The Limelight, he soon had DJing residences at MARS, Red Zone and MK and throwing outlaw club events known as DEEP . In 1990 he was hired by Cory Robins of Profile Records to work with VP Gary Pini as A&R scout. He has served as A&R director for Sm:)e communications and later went on to co-found the F-111 imprint.

Since 1992 DB has become known in the U.S. for pushing and promoting Drum & Bass, first with in 1992 his hardcore Breakbeat club NASA at The Shelter, (featured in the Larry Clark film Kids then with Gary Pini by launching Sm:)e communications for Profile Records and releasing the first Jungle singles and compilations in the U.S, as well as signing DJ Dara, thus kick starting his artist career. He and Dara then opened Breakbeat Science, dedicated to Drum & Bass. It was the first record store solely devoted to Drum & Bass in the U.S. In 2006 Breakbeat Science was responsible for the first compilation in the U.S. of the new sub genre of Drum & Bass, Dubstep.

In 1993 Gary Pini and DB were responsible for getting Robot Wars started by convincing Profile records to back the project, originally conceived by ex-Industrial Light & Magic model maker Mark Thorp, they staged the first live events in San Francisco.

In 2007 he released an artist album project called "Deep" with partner Stakka under the name Ror-Shak, focusing on pushing the limits on the more musical side of the D&B. The pair sold two of the songs to the CSI (franchise) before licensing the album to KOCH Records in the U.S & various EU labels.

Between 1994 and 2008 DB has released 13 mixed CDs.

In 1997 DB and Andrew Goldstone were hired by Warner Bros. Records to set up an electronic imprint, F-111 records. Two years into their contract, Ministry Of Sound poached the duo to head up A&R duties for the launch on an America version of the label.

In 2007, an essay by DJ DB was published in the book "Marooned: The Next Generation of Desert Island Discs" edited by Phil Freeman.

In 2010 DB, now using his full name DB Burkeman, expanded into another creative field by publishing a book on sticker art. DB had been collecting stickers since the 80's via punk rock & skate boarding, he and a partner (Monica LoCasio) created a history book, "Stickers- from Punk Rock to Contemporary Art" AKA Stuck-Up Piece Of Crap (for Rizzoli Publishing) on the subject of stickers, artists who've used the medium and their effect on popular culture. The pair are currently working towards touring the project as a museum quality exhibition for 2011. Stickers: From Punk Rock to Contemporary Art features the art of over 4000 stickers by more than 1300 artists.

He can be heard on the publicly funded online radio, Art International Radio on his weekly show called BLURRINGradio. The show is a "mixtape" of music, past & present that has, or is inspiring to him. The shows concept of a non genre, non decade specific show, was sparked by the fond memory of DB growing up listing to the late John Peel in London.

Source (edited): "http://en.wikipedia.org/wiki/DJ_DB"

Punk literature

Some of The Medway Poets in 2003: Bill Lewis, Sexton Ming, Robert Earl and Billy Childish

Punk literature (also called **punk lit** and, rarely, **punklit**) is a form of literature that emerged from the punk subculture. The attitude and ideology of punk rock gave rise to distinctive characteristics in the writing it manifested. It has had an influence on the popular transgressional fiction literary genre and several science fiction and fantasy genres have been derived from it.

Journalism

The punk rock subculture has had its own underground press in the form of punk zines, punk-related magazine circulations produced independently and with a highly limited reception and release. Punk zines chronicle and help to define punk in a particular area. Most punk scenes have at least one punk zine, which feature news, gossip, cultural criticism, and interviews with local or touring punk rock bands. Some punk zines take the form of perzines. Important punk zines include *Maximum RocknRoll*, *Punk Planet*, *Cometbus*, *Girl Germs*, *Kill Your Pet Puppy*, *J.D.s*, *Sniffin' Glue*, *Absolutely Zippo* and *Punk Magazine*. Punk journalists and magazine contributors include: Mykel Board, John Holmstrom, Robert Eggplant, Cristy C. Road and Aaron Cometbus.

Poetry

John Cooper Clarke in 1979

Punk poetry is perhaps the best recognized of traditional punk literature. Many punk poets are also musicians. Major punk poets include: Richard Hell, Jim Carroll, Patti Smith, John Cooper Clarke, Seething Wells, Raegan Butcher and Attila the Stockbroker. Jim Carroll's autobiographical works are among the first known examples of punk literature. The Medway Poets, a British punk performance group, was formed in 1979, and included punk musician Billy Childish. They are credited with influencing Tracey Emin, who was associated with them as a teenager. Members of the Medway Poets later formed the Stuckists art group.

A description by Charles Thomson of a Medway Poets performance contrasts with the sedate image of traditional poetry:

Bill Lewis jumped on a chair, threw his arms wide (at least once hitting his head on the ceiling) and pretended he was Jesus. Billy sprayed his poems over anyone too close to him and drank whisky excessively. Miriam told the world about her vagina. Rob and I did a joint performance posing, with little difficulty, as deranged, self-obsessed writers. Sexton finally introduced us to his girlfriend, Mildred, who turned out to be a wig on a wadge of newspaper on the end of an iron pipe.

Fiction

Punk has highly influenced the contemporary cyberpunk literary genre and its various derivatives. Punk zines have also spawned a considerable amount of punk-oriented fiction, some of which has made an impact outside of punk circles. Many of the major works of Kathy Acker reflect themes of punk literature, most notably *Blood and Guts in High School*. Daphne Gottlieb's poetic works are similar in motif. The novelist and screenwriter Diablo Cody has self-identified as "punk" in the past. *Love and Rockets* is a comic with a plot involving the Los Angeles punk scene.

Source (edited): "http://en.wikipedia.org/wiki/Punk_literature"

The Encyclopedia of Punk

The Encyclopedia of Punk is a reference book about punk rock written by Brian Cogan. The book's original title was the Encyclopedia of punk music and culture. The book traces the history of punk from its origins on the 1960s and 1970s to the present day. A large part of the book is made up of rare photos of bands.

Source (edited): "http://en.wikipedia.org/wiki/The_Encyclopedia_of_Punk"

Diablo Cody

Brook Busey (born June 14, 1978), better known by the pen name **Diablo Cody**, is an American screenwriter, writer, blogger, journalist, and author. She was first known for her candid chronicling of her year as a stripper in her *Pussy Ranch* blog and her 2006 memoir, *Candy Girl: A Year in the Life of an Unlikely Stripper*. Cody achieved critical acclaim worldwide for the script of the 2007 film *Juno*, winning the Academy Award for Best Original Screenplay.

A comedy-drama television series created by Cody, called *United States of Tara*, based on an idea by Steven Spielberg, was picked up for 12 episodes (including pilot) by the U.S. cable TV network Showtime, the Canadian channel The Movie Network and the Australian Broadcasting Corporation. After four episodes aired, the show was renewed for a second season. Two days after the second season premiere, it was renewed for a third season.

Early life and career

Cody and her older brother Marc were born and raised in Lemont, Illinois, a suburb of Chicago. Cody was raised Catholic and attended Benet Academy, a Roman Catholic school in Lisle, Illinois. She took the pen name Diablo Cody (*diablo* is Spanish for "devil") after repeatedly listening to the song *El Diablo* by Arcadia while passing through Cody, Wyoming. She graduated from the University of Iowa with a media studies degree. While at the University of Iowa, Cody was a DJ at KRUI 89.7 FM. She also worked in the acquisitions department in the main university library. Her first jobs were doing secretarial work at a Chicago law firm and later proofreading copy for advertisements that played on Twin Cities radio stations.

Cody began a parody of a weblog called *Red Secretary*, detailing the (fictional) exploits of a secretary living in Belarus. The events were thinly-veiled allegories for events that happened in Cody's real life, but told from the perspective of a disgruntled, English-idiom-challenged Eastern Bloc girl.

Cody's first *bona fide* blog appeared under the nickname *Darling Girl* after Cody had moved from Chicago to Minneapolis, Minnesota. Cody currently resides in Los Angeles and aspires to become a director.

Cody made a small cameo appearance as herself in the U.S. broadcast television series *90210* (2008). She appeared in the same episode that marked the return of Tori Spelling as Donna Martin, in which Cody needed Spelling's character to make a dress for a red carpet event.

She is currently writing, producing, and hosting the YouTube-based web series, *Red Band Trailer*, which she created alongside husband Dan Maurio. Cody interviews celebrities, that have included Adam Brody, Chelsea Handler, Megan Fox, Jason Bateman, and Kyle Chandler, both in a trailer and at her poolside tiki bar. The channel currently has over 4,000 subscribers and the videos have been watched over 750,000 times.

On April 6, 2010, Cody announced that she was expecting her first child with her husband Dan Maurio, who works on *Chelsea Lately*. The couple married in the summer of 2009. Their son Marcello Daniel Maurio was born July 27, 2010. Cody also appears frequently as a "roundtable" guest on *Chelsea Lately*.

Stripping and journalism

On a whim, Cody signed up for amateur night at a Minneapolis strip club called the Skyway Lounge. Enjoying the experience, she eventually quit her day job and took up stripping full-time. Cody also spent time working peep shows at Sex World, a Minneapolis adult novelty and DVD store. Cody soon made a retreat to journalism and a budding writing career stimulated by her skin trade days.

While still stripping, Cody began writing for *City Pages*, an alternative Twin Cities weekly newspaper. She left *City Pages* just before it changed editorial hands. Cody has since written for the now-defunct *Jane* magazine. In December 2007, Cody debuted as *Entertainment Weekly* magazine's newest columnist, joining regular contributors Mark Harris and the iconic pop horror author Stephen King on a rotational basis.

At the age of 24, Cody wrote her memoir *Candy Girl: A Year in the Life of an Unlikely Stripper*. The memoir began after Mason Novick, who would soon become Cody's manager, showed interest in Cody's sharp and sarcastic voice. Based on the popularity *Pussy Ranch* had received, he was able to secure her a publishing contract with Gotham Books.

Screenwriting

Cody, January 2008

After completion of her book, Cody was encouraged by Mason Novick to write her first screenplay. Within months she wrote *Juno*, a coming-of-age story about a teenager's unplanned pregnancy. The Jason Reitman-directed comedy stars Ellen Page and Michael Cera.

In July 2007, Showtime announced that it would be producing a pilot of Cody's Dreamworks television series, *United States of Tara*. Based on an idea by Steven Spielberg, *Tara* is a comedy about a mother with dissociative identity disorder, starring Toni Collette. The series began filming in Spring 2008, and premiered on January 18, 2009.

In October 2007, Cody sold a script titled *Girly Style* to Universal Studios, and a horror script called *Jennifer's Body* to Fox Atomic. Released on September 18, 2009, *Jennifer's Body* starred Megan Fox as the title character. Cody also partially wrote the script for *Burlesque*, a musical film by director/screenwriter Steven Antin.

Cody is good friends with fellow screenwriters Dana Fox (*What Happens in Vegas*, *Couples Retreat*) and Lorene Scafaria (*Nick and Norah's Infinite Playlist*) and they often write their screenplays while hanging out together, in order to get advice from one another.

Variety has reported that Cody will be adapting the *Sweet Valley High* book series into a movie. Cody will also produce the film adaptation with her manager, Mason Novick, Adam Siegel and Marc Platt.

It was announced on July 13, 2011 that Cody was being brought in to revise the script for the upcoming remake of the horror classic, The Evil Dead.

Nominations and awards

Juno was runner-up for the Toronto International Film Festival People's Choice Award, won second prize at the Rome Film Festival, and earned four Academy Award nominations, including one for Best Picture. Cody herself won an Academy Award for Best Original Screenplay for her debut script, which also picked up a Golden Globe nomination and an Independent Spirit Award for Best Screenplay. She also won screenplay honors from BAFTA, the Writers Guild of America, Broadcast Film Critics Association, the National Board of Review, the Chicago Film Critics Association, the Dallas-Fort Worth Film Critics Association, the Florida Film Critics Circle, the Southeastern Film Critics Association, the Satellite Awards, and the Cinema for Peace Award 2008 for Most Valuable Work of Director, Producer & Screenwriter for *Juno*.

Source (edited): "http://en.wikipedia.org/wiki/Diablo_Cody"

Kathy Acker

Kathy Acker (née **Karen Lehmann**) (18 April 1947 – 30 November 1997) was an American experimental novelist, punk poet, playwright, essayist, postmodernist and sex-positive feminist writer. She was strongly influenced by the Black Mountain School, William S. Burroughs, David Antin, French critical theory, philosophy, and pornography.

Biography

The daughter of Donald and Claire (Weill) Lehman, a wealthy Jewish family, Kathy Acker was born in New York City on April 18. There is some question as to her year of birth, however: the Library of Congress lists her birth year as 1948, a few sources have listed 1947, but most obituaries state that she was born in 1944. The pregnancy was unplanned, and Donald Lehman abandoned the family before Kathy was born; Acker's relationship with her domineering mother even into adulthood was fraught with hostility and anxiety because Acker felt unloved and unwanted. Her mother soon remarried, a union that Acker later characterized as an essentially passionless marriage to an ineffectual man, and Acker was raised in her mother and stepfather's respectable upper-middle-class Jewish home on New York's Upper East Side.

As a girl, Acker was expected to act with ladylike propriety in this oppressive, well-to-do environment, yet she was fascinated by pirates, a fascination that continued until the end of her life. She wanted to grow up to be a pirate, but she knew that only men could be pirates. Thus Acker experienced early the limitations of gender. However, she found that reading about pirates was a way of running away from home, and she turned to books as her reality. She associated reading and writing with bodily pleasure and remained a voracious reader throughout her life.

Acker took her last name from her first husband, Robert Acker; though named Karen, she was known as Kathy by her friends and family. She studied classics as an undergraduate at Brandeis University and aspired to write novels but moved to San Diego to further pursue her studies. Acker's first work appeared in print as part of the burgeoning New York literary underground of the mid-1970s. She claimed that her early writings were profoundly influenced by her experiences working for a few months as a stripper. She remained on the margins of the literary establishment, only being published by small presses until the mid-1980s, thus earning herself the epithet of literary terrorist. 1984 saw her first British publication, a novel called *Blood and Guts in High School*. From here on Acker produced a considerable body of novels, almost all still in print with Grove Press. She wrote pieces for a number of magazines and anthologies, and also had notable pieces printed in issues of *RE/Search*, *Angel Exhaust* and *Rapid Eye*. Towards the end of her life she had a measure of success in the conventional press—the *Guardian* newspaper published several of her articles, including an interview with the Spice Girls, which she submitted just a few months before her death.

Acker's formative influences were American poets and writers (the Black Mountain poets, especially Jackson Mac Low, Charles Olson, William S. Burroughs), and the Fluxus movement, as well as literary theory, especially the French feminists and Gilles Deleuze. In her work, she combined plagiarism, cut-up techniques, pornography, autobiography, persona and personal essay to confound expectations of what fiction should be. She acknowledged the performative function of language in drawing attention to the instability of female identity in male narrative and literary history (*Don Quixote*), created parallelism in characters and autobiographical personas and experimented with pronouns, upsetting conventional syntax.

In *In Memoriam to Identity*, Acker draws attention to popular analyses of Rimbaud's life and *The Sound and the Fury*, constructing or revealing social and literary identity. Though she was known in the literary world for creating a whole new style of feminist prose and for her transgressive fiction, she was also a punk and feminist icon for her devoted portrayals of subcultures, strong-willed women, and violence.

In April 1996 Acker was diagnosed with breast cancer and had a double mastectomy. In January 1997 she wrote about her loss of faith in conventional medicine in a *Guardian* article, "The Gift of Disease." In the article she explains that after unsuccessful surgery, which left her feeling physically mutilated and emotionally debilitated, she rejected the passivity of the patient in the medical mainstream and began to seek out the advice of nutritionists, acupuncturists, psychic healers, and Chinese herbalists. She found appealing the claim that instead of being an object of knowledge, as in Western medicine, the patient becomes a seer, a seeker of wisdom, that illness becomes the teacher and the patient the student. After pursuing several forms of alternative medicine in England and the United States, Acker died a year and a half later from complications of breast cancer in an alternative cancer clinic in Tijuana, Mexico. She died in Room 101, to which her friend Alan Moore quipped, "There's nothing that woman can't turn into a literary reference."

Literary overview

Born and raised in New York City, novelist, poet and performance artist Kathy Acker came to be closely associated with the punk movement of the 1970s and '80s that affected much of the culture in and around Manhattan. As an adult, however, she moved around quite a bit. She received her bachelor's degree from the University of California, San Diego in 1968; there she worked with David Antin and Jerome Rothenberg.

She did two years worth of graduate work at City University of New York in Classics, specializing in Greek, but left before earning a degree. While still in New York she worked as a file clerk, secretary, stripper, and porn performer. During the 1970s she often moved back and forth between San Diego, San Francisco and New York.

She married twice, and though most of her relationships were with men, she was openly bisexual for at least part of her adult life. In 1979 she won the Pushcart Prize for her short story "New York City in 1979." During the early 1980s she lived in London, where she wrote several of her most critically acclaimed works. After returning to the United States in the late 1980s she worked as an adjunct professor at the San Francisco Art Institute for about six years and as a visiting professor at several universities, including the University of Idaho, the University of California, San Diego, University of California, Santa Barbara, the California Institute of Arts, and Roanoke College.

Acker's controversial body of work borrows heavily from the experimental styles of William S. Burroughs and Marguerite Duras. She often used extreme forms of pastiche and even Burroughs's cut-up technique, in which one cuts passages and sentences into several pieces and rearranges them somewhat randomly. Acker herself situated her writing within a post-nouveau roman European tradition. In her texts, she combines biographical elements, power, sex and violence. Indeed, critics often compare her writing to that of Alain Robbe-Grillet and Jean Genet. Critics have noticed links to Gertrude Stein and photographers Cindy Sherman and Sherrie Levine. Acker's novels also exhibit a fascination with and an indebtedness to tattoos. She even dedicated *Empire of the Senseless* to her tattooist.

Although associated with generally well-respected artists, even Acker's most recognized novels, *Blood and Guts in High School*, *Great Expectations* and *Don Quixote* receive mixed critical attention. Most critics acknowledge Acker's skilled manipulation of plagiarized texts from writers as varied as Charles Dickens, Marcel Proust, and Marquis de Sade.

Feminist critics have also had strong responses both for and against Acker's writing. While some praise her for exposing a misogynistic capitalist society that uses sexual domination as a key form of oppression, others argue that her extreme and frequent use of violent sexual imagery quickly becomes numbing and leads to the degrading objectification of women. Despite repeated criticisms, Acker maintained that in order to challenge the phallogocentric power structures of language, literature must not only experiment with syntax and style, but also give voice to the silenced subjects that common taboos marginalize. The inclusion of controversial topics such as abortion, rape, incest, terrorism, pornography, graphic violence, and feminism demonstrate that conviction.

Acker published her first book, *Politics*, in 1972. Although the collection of poems and essays did not garner much critical or public attention, it did establish her reputation within the New York punk scene. In 1973 she published her first novel *The Childlike Life of the Black Tarantula: Some Lives of Murderesses* under the pseudonym Black Tarantula. In 1974 she published her second novel, *I Dreamt I Was a Nymphomaniac: Imagining*.

In 1979 Acker finally reccived popular attention when she won a Pushcart Prize for her short story "New York City in 1979." She did not receive critical attention, however, until she published *Great Expectations* in 1982. The opening of *Great Expectations* is a clear rewriting of Charles Dickens's classic of the same name. It features Acker's usual subject matter, including a semi-autobiographical account of her mother's suicide and the appropriation of several other texts, including Pierre Guyotat's violent and sexually explicit "Eden Eden Eden". That same year, Acker published a chapbook titled *Hello, I'm Erica Jong*.

Acker wrote the script for the 1983 film *Variety*, directed by Bette Gordon with actors including Nan Goldin, Will

Patton, and Luis Guzmán.

Despite the increased recognition she got for *Great Expectations*, *Blood and Guts in High School* is often considered Acker's breakthrough work. Published in 1984, it is one of her most extreme explorations of sexuality and violence. Borrowing from, among other texts, Nathaniel Hawthorne's *The Scarlet Letter*, *Blood and Guts* details the experiences of Janey Smith, a sex addicted and pelvic-inflammatory-disease-ridden urbanite who is in love with a father who sells her into slavery. Many critics criticized it for being demeaning toward women, and Germany banned it completely. Acker published the German court judgment against *Blood and Guts in High School* in *Hannibal Lecter, My Father*.

In 1984 Acker published *My Death My Life by Pier Paolo Pasolini* and a year later published *Algeria: A Series of Invocations because Nothing Else Works*. In 1986 she published *Don Quixote*, another one of her more acclaimed novels. In Acker's version of Miguel de Cervantes' classic, Don Quixote becomes a young woman obsessed with poststructuralist theory, taking it to a nihilistic extreme. Moreover, the Don's insanity that causes her to wander the streets of St. Petersburg & New York City was caused from having an abortion. She recognizes the world's many lies and fakes, believes in nothing and regards identity as an internalized fictional construct. Marching around New York City and London with her dog St. Simeon, who serves as her Sancho Panza, Don Quixote attacks the sexist societies while simultaneously deflating feminist mythologies.

Acker published *Empire of the Senseless* in 1988 and considered it a turning point in her writing. While she still borrows from other texts, including Mark Twain's *The Adventures of Huckleberry Finn*, the plagiarism is less obvious. However, one of Acker's more controversial plagiarisms is from William Gibson's 1984 text "Neuromancer" in which Acker equates code with the female body and its militaristic implications. The novel comes from the voices of two terrorists, Abhor, who is half human and half robot, and her lover Thivai. The story takes place in the decaying remnants of a post-revolutionary Paris. Like her other works, *Empire of the Senseless* includes graphic violence and sexuality. However, it turns toward concerns of language more than her previous works. In 1988 she also published *Literal Madness: Three Novels* which included three previously published works: *Florida* deconstructs and reduces John Huston's 1948 film noir classic *Key Largo* into its base sexual politics, *Kathy Goes to Haiti* details a young woman's relationship and sexual exploits while on vacation, and *My Death My Life by Pier Paolo Pasolini* provides a fictional *autobiography* of the Italian filmmaker in which he solves his own murder.

Between 1990 and 1993 Acker published four more books: *In Memoriam to Identity* (1990); *Hannibal Lecter, My Father* (1991); *Portrait of an Eye: Three Novels* (1992), also composed of already published works; and *My Mother: Demonology* (1992). Many critics complained that these later works became redundant and predictable, as Acker continued to explore the same taboos in a similar fashion. Her last novel, *Pussy, King of the Pirates*, published in 1996, showed signs of Acker's broadening interests as it incorporates more humor, lighter fantasy and a consideration of Eastern texts and philosophy that was largely absent in her earlier works.

Posthumous reputation

Acker's work has been acknowledged by a number of younger writers working in an experimental style, including Stewart Home, Mark Amerika, Barry Graham, Anna Joy Springer, Tribe 8 singer and writer Lynn Breedlove, Alexander Laurence, Tamil novelist Charu Nivedita, Noah Cicero, Travis Jeppesen, and Salvador Plascencia. Kathleen Hanna of Bikini Kill and Kim Gordon, co-founder of Sonic Youth have also acknowledged her influence.

Three volumes of her non-fiction have been published and re-published since her death. In 2002 New York University (NYU) staged *Discipline and Anarchy*, a retrospective exhibition of her works, while in 2008 London's Institute of Contemporary Arts held an evening of her films. Recently (2007) Amandla Publishing has re-published Acker's articles for the *New Statesman* from 1989 to 1991.

Quotes

- "We don't have a clue what it is to be male or female, or if there are intermediate genders. Male and female might be fields which overlap into androgyny or different kinds of sexual desires. But because we live in a Western, patriarchal world, we have very little chance of exploring these gender possibilities."
- "Literature is that which denounces and slashes apart the repressing machine at the level of the signified."
- "The students who come to my class are very closely related to all the evil girls who are very interested in their bodies and sex and pleasure. I learn a lot from them about how to have pleasure and how cool the female body is. One of my students had a piercing through her labia. And she told me about how when you ride on a motorcycle, the little bead on the ring acts like a vibrator. Her story turned me on so I did it. I got two. It was very cool. I'm very staid compared to my students, actually. I come from a generation where you've got the PC dykes and confused heterosexuals. No one ever told me that you could walk around with a strap-on, having orgasms."
- "Let's compare a pencil to a vagina."

Published works

- *Politics* (1972)
- *Childlike Life of the Black Tarantula By the Black Tarantula* (1973)
- *I Dreamt I Was a Nymphomaniac: Imagining* (1974)
- *Adult Life of Toulouse Lautrec* (1978)
- *Florida* (1978)
- *Kathy Goes To Haiti* (1978)
- *N.Y.C. in 1979* (1981)

- *Great Expectations* (1983)
- *Algeria : A Series of Invocations Because Nothing Else Works* (1984)
- *Blood and Guts in High School* (1984)
- *Don Quixote: Which Was a Dream* (1986)
- *Literal Madness: Three Novels* (Reprinted 1987)
- *My Death My Life by Pier Paolo Pasolini*
- *Wordplays 5 : An Anthology of New American Drama* (1987)
- *Empire of the Senseless* (1988)
- *In Memoriam to Identity* (1990)
- *Hannibal Lecter, My Father* (1991)
- *My Mother: Demonology* (1994)
- *Pussycat Fever* (1995)
- *Dust. Essays* (1995)
- *Pussy, King of the Pirates* (1996)
- *Bodies of Work : Essays* (1997)
- *Portrait of an Eye: Three Novels* (Reprinted 1998)
- *Redoing Childhood* (2000) spoken word CD, KRS 349.
- "Rip-Off Red, Girl Detective" (pub. 2002 from manuscript of 1973)

Source (edited): "http://en.wikipedia.org/wiki/Kathy_Acker"

Aaron Cometbus

Aaron Elliott (born May 20, 1968), better known as **Aaron Cometbus**, is an American drummer, lyricist, self-described "punk anthropologist," novelist, and author of punk rock zine *Cometbus*.

Personal life

Born in Berkeley, California, Cometbus started writing fanzines in 1981 with Jesse Michaels (later of Operation Ivy and Common Rider) and started his own after Michaels moved to Pennsylvania in October 1981. Cometbus became an active participant in the Gilman Street Project and was a founding member of Crimpshrine, a highly influential East Bay punk rock band which also featured Jeff Ott. After the demise of Crimpshrine, Cometbus formed Pinhead Gunpowder with a handful of people from the East Bay punk scene, including Mike Kirsch, Jason White and Billie Joe Armstrong of Green Day. He also toured as a roadie with Green Day a few times and played drums for a few shows. He has played in a multitude of short-lived bands that generally release just a seven-inch or two before breaking up (see Band history).

He is a co-owner of the used bookstore in Williamsburg, Brooklyn, Book Thug Nation.

Cometbus zine

Cometbus is most famous for publishing the zine *Cometbus*, which he began in Berkeley, California in 1981. Cometbus has self-published the usually-handwritten zine ever since, despite a few breaks. The name *Cometbus* was coined by Gregg Turkington during the early days of the magazine when the name changed from issue to issue. *Cometbus* consisted of band interviews, personal diaries, artwork, and observations on the punk subculture in the San Francisco Bay Area and beyond. The zine captured a slice of life in Oakland and Berkeley, California from the late 1980s through the 1990s. This includes squatting, collective living, falling in love and other perils of the punk rock lifestyle. Cometbus's writing is characterized by stories of loneliness and alienation, tempered with episodes of brightness and perennial hope in the ability of humans to connect to one another.

Cometbus has a very identifiable aesthetic: the author almost always uses black and white, and uses his photocopier as a tool for distorting and manipulating images and text. His handwritten print, in which almost all of the zine's issues are written, is very identifiable and is often closely associated with the zine. This aesthetic follows Cometbus to his bands, where he often does the layouts and artwork.

On August 1, 2002, Last Gasp Publishing released *Despite Everything: A Cometbus Omnibus* (Last Gasp of San Francisco; September 2002, ISBN 0-86719-561-4), a 608-page compendium of selections from 43 early *Cometbus* issues which are long out of print and often difficult to find.

From 2004 to 2006, Cometbus took a hiatus from writing *Cometbus* to pursue publishing his writing through other channels. *Cometbus* came out of retirement in 2006 with the release of *Cometbus #50*, the 25th anniversary issue of the magazine, which features interviews, short stories, book store reviews, and more of its usual type of content.

Cometbus #51, The Loneliness of the Electric Menorah, was released in September 2008. It chronicles the history of Moe's Books and other longtime businesses on Telegraph Avenue in Berkeley, California.

Cometbus #52, The Spirit of St-Louis, Or, How to Break Your Own Heart, A Tragedy in 24 Parts, was released in 2009. Cometbus says in his blurb: "It all starts with the story I've told so many times it's turned stale and tired from overuse. There I was, dropped off in a city far from home. I didn't know a soul or have a hope, and so on..." Both issue #52 of *Cometbus* and the novel *I Wish There Was Something That I Could Quit* are rumored to be about his stay and relationships in Pensacola, Florida.

Cometbus #53 features contributions from Maddalena Poletta and a cover by Eisner Award winner Nate Powell. Released in 2009, it features a lengthy piece on art, comics, and the early days of punk in NYC in the mid-1970s that is largely derived from an in-depth interview Cometbus conducted with John Holstrom, the co-founder of the legendary Punk Magazine.

Cometbus #54, In China with Green Day, released in February 2011, is about Cometbus' and Green Day's tour of Asia in 2010. Oddly enough, considering the title, they do not make it to mainland China at any point.

Other writing

In addition to writing for his own zine, Cometbus has contributed stories to several other zines such as *Absolutely*

Zippo, *Maximumrocknroll*, and *Tales of Blarg*, occasionally writing under the pseudonym Skrub. His work is easily recognizable by his distinctive, block-lettered handwritten script. His handwriting also appears in the liner notes of early Green Day albums and Jawbreaker's *Etc.* compilation.

Double Duce (Last Gasp, 2003, ISBN 0-86719-586-X) is a novel based on Cometbus's life in a punk house called Double Duce, and collects material published in *Cometbus* issues 32, 35, 37, 38, 41, 42, 43, and 45.

A novel titled *I Wish There Was Something That I Could Quit*, was published on March 15, 2006. This novel was loosely based on his experiences in Pensacola, Florida during the start of the Iraq War and is arguably his most political work.

He has also released a few smaller collections of short stories, *Mixed Reviews* and *Chicago Stories* (self published, 2004), a small collection about Chicago originally published in "Cometbus" issues 35, 37, 38, 41, and 45.

Two collections have been translated into French, including *En dépit de tout* (1997). *Double Duce* has been translated into German and was published by Lautsprecherverlag as "Doppelzwei" in 2004.

Band history

- S.A.G. (East Bay CA; 1982–1984)
- Crimpshrine (East Bay CA; 1984–1989)
- Screeching Weasel (Chicago, IL; 1988 (two shows))
- Sweet Baby (a.k.a. Sweet Baby Jesus) (East Bay/Northern CA; 1989–1990)
- Pinhead Gunpowder (East Bay CA; 1991–2001; 2008, 2010)
- Mundt (Northern CA; 1992)
- Strawman (San Francisco, CA; 1993?)
- Shotwell (San Francisco CA; a.k.a. Shotwell Coho) (1994)
- EFS (Berkeley CA; 1995)
- Cosmetic Puffs (Eureka, Ca; 1995)
- Redmond Shooting Stars (Eugene, OR; 1995–1996)
- Cleveland Bound Death Sentence (Minneapolis MN; 1997–1998; 2004)
- The Retard Beaters (Chattanooga, TN; 1997–1998)
- Harbinger (with Robert Eggplant, formerly of Blatz, and John Geek of Fleshies) (East Bay CA; 1997–2001)
- The Blank Fight (with Rymodee of This Bike Is a Pipe Bomb) (Pensacola FL; 1999–2000)
- Astrid Oto (Asheville NC; 1999–2001)
- Colbom (San Francisco CA; 2001)
- End of the World News (New York; 2002–2003)
- Crybaby MacArthur (Brooklyn NY; 2004–2006)
- The Thorns of Life (with Blake Schwarzenbach and Daniela Sea) (Brooklyn NY; 2008–2009)
- Scooby Don't
- T. Zatana
- This Bike Is a Pipe Bomb

Source (edited): "http://en.wikipedia.org/wiki/Aaron_Cometbus"

Absolutely Zippo

Absolutely Zippo is a punk rock fanzine created by Robert Eggplant to document the happenings of the East Bay Berkeley punk scene during its heyday in the late 1980s/early 1990s. Contributors included Aaron Cometbus of Cometbus fame (writing under the pen name "Skrub"), Billie Joe Armstrong of Green Day (who wrote 2 brief articles about how to be a couch potato) and Larry Livermore of Lookout! Records.

Absolutely Zippo was known for scene reports, record and show reviews, band photos (often grainy and low-quality due to cheap photocopying), stories, comics, rants, editorials, artwork and more. The 16th issue, released in 1992, was accompanied by the cassette tape compilation *Later The Same Year*, which included songs by bands such as Filth, Gru'ups, Spitboy, Jack Acid, Good Grief, Downfall, Grimple, Monsula, Chicken Head and many others. It was later reissued on SPAM Records in CD format. *Absolutely Zippo* was unique in that Robert Eggplant was a member of the bands Blatz, The Hope Bombs and more recently Harbinger, as well as a volunteer at 924 Gilman Street, and so offered an inside, on the frontlines view of the punk scene.

In 2000, *Absolutely Zippo* was complied and released in paperback form. This volume is entitled *Absolutely Zippo: Anthology of a Fanzine 1989 - 1998*. Since that time over ten issues have been released including one issue made from paper rescued by 'dumpster diving'.

Source (edited): "http://en.wikipedia.org/wiki/Absolutely_Zippo"

Black Market Magazine

Black Market Magazine was a music, film, art and comic zine which started in 1985.

Based in San Diego, Black Market Magazine initially featured mostly reviews / interviews of punk rock and other alternative bands such as Samhain, The Cramps, D.O.A., Tex and the Horseheads, G.B.H., New Order, Christian Death, Bad Religion, Ramones, Murphey's Law, Butthole Surfers, Wasted Youth, Danzig, Marilyn Manson, etc... However over its 13 issue / 10 year lifespan, film and art would fill the majority of its pages. Interviews would now include sci-fi film historian / former editor of Famous Monsters of Filmland Forrest J. Ackerman along with actors and directors such as Bill Paxton, Adam Rifkin, Wayne Newton, Jeffrey

Levy. Issues would also showcase artists such as R.K. Sloane, Jeff Gaither, Pizz, Lee Ellingson, Drew Elliot, Roman Dirge (Lenore Comix), GUF, Peter Bagge (Hate Comix), Brian Clarke, Michael Gilbert (Mr. Monster) and many others.

Source (edited): "http://en.wikipedia.org/wiki/Black_Market_Magazine"

Burnt Offering

Burnt Offering was a punk fanzine based in and around Northampton, England, from 1979 to 1980.

In keeping with the DIY style of the time, *Burnt Offering*'s house style was a mixture of badly-typed articles, ransom note effect lettering and cartoon drawings. Its content included interviews, rants, reviews and news of forthcoming gigs.

Burnt Offering ran for twelve issues, sold for 10 pence and was available via clothes shops and record shops.

In 2006 The Isaws, who had been a prominent local band interviewed by B.O. in 1979, released a demo CD titled *Burnt Offering*.

Source (edited): "http://en.wikipedia.org/wiki/Burnt_Offering"

Chainsaw (punk zine)

Chainsaw fanzine no.2, September/October 1977

Chainsaw, a punk zine edited by "Charlie Chainsaw" was published in suburban Croydon in 1977 and ran to fourteen issues before ceasing publication in 1984. A hand-lettered 'n' became a stylised trademark in articles after the 'n' key broke on the editor's typewriter. In addition to a free flexi disc promoting two or three up-and-coming punk bands, 1980s issues featured cartoon strips and two innovative colour covers by Michael J. Weller. 1970s issues featured the cartoon strip 'Hitler's Kids', authored by Andrew Marr using punk nom-de-plume "Willy D" at the beginning of his successful journalistic career. Charlie Chainsaw formed the band Rancid Hell Spawn when the punk zine discontinued.

Source (edited): "http://en.wikipedia.org/wiki/Chainsaw_(punk_zine)"

Death To The World

Death To The World is an Eastern Orthodox zine.

History

Death to the World was started by monks and nuns from the St Herman of Alaska Monastery in Platina, California, as a medium of evangelism to teens involved in the punk subculture by monastics who were ex-punks. A founding member was Justin Marler who, soon after recording *Volume One* with seminal doom metal band Sleep in 1991, left for seven years of monastic life while Sleep went on to become metal icons.

Originally, the monastics planned to submit an article about Fr. Seraphim Rose to the magazine *Maximum RocknRoll*. They later decided to try to place an ad for their monastery, but were only rudely rejected, being told that the magazine "only [ran] ads for music and zines". This inspired them to begin a zine.

The first issue was printed in the December of '94 featuring a monk holding a skull on cover. The hand-drawn bold letters across the top read "DEATH TO THE WORLD, The Last True Rebellion" and the back cover held the caption: "they hated me without a cause." ... The first issue, decorated with ancient icons and lives of martyrs inside, was advertised in Maximum RocknRoll and brought letters from all around the world.

The 'zine continued to be published and distributed at punks shows and underground hangouts. It was estimated that at one time, there were 50,000 in circulation. The monastics put out 12 issues in all, after which they continued distributing the 'zine but didn't publish new issues.

Eight years later, the zine was revived by convert members of Saint Barnabas Antiochian Orthodox Church in Costa Mesa, California. New issues are submitted to the St Herman monks for editing and revision, and are released quarterly.

The zine had a considerable impact on counter culture youth during the mid to late 90s, which caught the attention of mainstream press, and quickly led to the release of Justin Marler's first book in 1997, Youth of the Apocalypse, (co-authored with a fellow monastic).
Source (edited): "http://en.wikipedia.org/wiki/Death_To_The_World"

Flipside (fanzine)

Flipside was a punk rock fanzine published in Los Angeles, California from 1977 to 2000.

Flipside, issue 6, 1978.

As one of the first and longest running US punk rock fanzines, this publication extensively chronicled the world of independent and underground music during this era. Known for its highly opinionated cast of writers, *Flipside* evolved from cheaply printed to glossy cover. Their articles extended to coverage of the UFO phenomenon, drugs, and independent film.

Flipside fanzine put on a Burning Man-style festival, in California's Mojave Desert at a location known as Jawbone Canyon for several years during the mid 1990s. It was much smaller and more localized than the actual Burning Man Festivals and often featured bands that Flipside put out on their own label. Special guests included Fugazi, The Offspring and Nik Turner, of Hawkwind fame.

Recording

For several years, the publishers also produced punk rock records under the Flipside label. Bands on its own label included Detox, Doggy Style, Bulimia Banquet, Anti-Scrunti Faction, Sluts for Hire, Popdefect, Paper Tulips, Sandy Duncan's Eye, and Babyland. Some of the most sought after of Flipside releases are the Flipside Video Fanzine series released in the early 1980s which were collections of performances of punk bands such as Black Flag, Agent Orange, TSOL, Social Distortion, etc.

Flipside Records released the first Beck recordings; a split 7" with the band Bean plus the full length CD *Stereopathetic Soulmanure*.
Source (edited): "http://en.wikipedia.org/wiki/Flipside_(fanzine)"

Homocore (zine)

Homocore is an American anarcho-punk zine created by Tom Jennings and Deke Nihilson, and published in San Francisco from 1988 to 1991. One of the first queer zines, *Homocore* was directed toward the hardcore punk youth of the gay underground. The publication has been noted for popularizing the Queercore movement on the United States west coast.

History

The word 'homocore' was first coined by G.B. Jones and Bruce LaBruce in the Toronto-based queer punk zine, *J.D.s*. The term was a neologism based upon combining the words homosexual and hardcore, and used as a description of their audience: disenfranchised queer hardcore punks. The word first appeared in *J.D.'s* issue #1 in 1985.

Tom Jennings borrowed the word 'homocore' after he and co-editor Deke Nihilson met Jones and LaBruce at the 1987 Anarchist Survival Gathering in Toronto. Inspired by the editors of *J.D.'s*, and other anarchists, Jennings and Nihilson returned to San Francisco and began the *Homocore* zine. The first issue was published in September 1988. Although their initial audience was the queer underground within the San Francisco area, letters published in later issues came from readers around the world. *Homocore* featured writers, artists and bands such as the Anarcho-punk group The Apostles, photographer Daniel Nicoletta, Chainsaw Records label owner and musician Donna Dresch, writer and founder of Lookout Records Larry Livermore, Bruce LaBruce and G.B. Jones. Steve Abbott first published excerpts of what would become the novel *The Lizard Club* in *Homocore*. Writing for *The Village Voice*, author Dennis Cooper started off his 1990 survey of the then-nascent queer zine scene with a review of this zine, noting "Homocore is the most generous and info-packed of the zines."

Subsequently, eight issues were published over a 16 month period, ending in February 1991. An odd issue, titled *Bad Poetry* Issue #5½, resulted from the use of overlarge newsprint paper. The editors also organized *Homocore* events in which bands such as Fugazi, MDC, Beat Happening and Comrades In Arms appeared. The 1991 short film *Shred Of Sex* by Greta Snider was made at *Homocore* headquarters.

Influence and cultural significance

Homocore has been noted as being instrumental in popularizing the Queercore movement, especially on the west coast of North America. In the book *DIY: The Rise and Fall of Lo-Fi Culture*, Amy Spencer stated that "zines acknowledged that their origins stemmed directly from the existence of J.D.s and Homocore." Spencer further wrote that *Homocore* and similar zines became "required reading material" for those disillusioned by other more mainstream gay choices.

In his book examining zines, Stephen Duncombe explains, "Queer punk rockers, for example, feel unrepresented in both predominantly straight punk zines and the liberal assimilationist gay and lesbian press. Therefore they use zines like *Homocore* and *J.D.s* as virtual meeting places, spaces to define and communicate who they are, and remind themselves (and others) that they are not alone." Christopher Wilde in an 2007 essay for Queer Life said it was *Homocore'* #7, the final issue, which is the "most fondly remembered of all queer zines" and "cemented its reputation as a leader in the evolution of the [radical queer] scene."

Issues

- *Homocore* #1, September 1988
- *Homocore* #2, December 1988
- *Homocore* #3, February 1989
- *Homocore* #4, June 1989
- *Homocore* #5, December 1989
- *Homocore* #5½
- *Homocore* #6, May 1990
- *Homocore* #7, February 1991

Source (edited): "http://en.wikipedia.org/wiki/Homocore_(zine)"

J.D.s

J.D.s is a queer punk zine founded in Toronto by G.B. Jones and co-published with Bruce LaBruce, that ran for eight issues from 1985 to 1991.

" *J.D.s* is seen by many to be the catalyst that pushed the queercore scene into existence", writes Amy Spencer in *DIY: The Rise of Lo-Fi Culture*. Writing in the journal *C: International Contemporary Art*, Earl Miller calls J.D.s "tremendously influential."

After the initial release of the first few issues of *J.D.s*, the editors wrote a manifesto called "Don't Be Gay" which was featured in *Maximum RocknRoll* zine. According to Amy Spencer, "The article appeared in February 1989 and simultaneously attacked both punk and gay subcultures..." G.B Jones states, "Our goal, vis-à-vis the punk scene, was to antagonize." Spencer continues, "Following their article, a queer punk culture did begin to emerge."

The editors had initially chosen the appellation "homocore" to describe the movement they began, but later replaced the word 'homo' with 'queer' to create Queercore, to better reflect the diversity of the scene and to disassociate themselves completely from the oppressive confines of the gay and lesbian communities' orthodoxy and agenda. G.B. Jones says, "We were just as eager to provoke the gays and lesbians as we were the punks." According to Bruce LaBruce, *J.D.s* initially stood for Juvenile Delinquents, but "also encompassed such youth cult icons as James Dean and J.D. Salinger."

The zine featured the photos and the "Tom Girl" drawings of G.B. Jones, stories by Bruce LaBruce, and the "J.D.s Top Ten Homocore Hits", a list of queer-themed songs such as "Off-Duty Sailor" by The Dicks, "Only Loved At Night" by The Raincoats, "Gimme Gimme Gimme (My Man After Midnight)" by The Leather Nun, "Homophobia" by Victims Family, "I, Bloodbrothers Be" by Shock Headed Peters, "The Anal Staircase" by Coil and many more. Groups like Anti-Scrunti Faction were featured in the fanzine. Contributors included Donny the Punk, comic artist Anonymous Boy, author Dennis Cooper, artist Carrie McNinch, musician Anita Smith, punk drag performer Vaginal Davis and Klaus and Jena von Brücker.

Zines such as *Homocore* and *Fanorama*, among others, credit *J.D.s* with inspiring them to begin publishing.

In 1990, *J.D.s* released the first compilation of queercore songs, a cassette tape entitled *J.D.s Top Ten Homocore Hit Parade Tape*, which featured the groups The Apostles, Academy 23 and No Brain Cells from the UK, Fifth Column, Zuzu's Petals and Toilet Slaves from Canada, Bomb, Big Man, Robt. Omlit and Nikki Parasite of The Parasites from the U.S. and, from New Zealand, Gorse.

Also in 1990, and '91, G.B. Jones and Bruce LaBruce began presenting *J.D.s* movie nights . These happened in London in the UK, in San Francisco, and at Hallwalls in Buffalo in the U.S., and in Montreal, and Toronto in Canada with the editors and various contributors showing films, all made on extremely low budgets on Super 8 film, such as Jones' *The Troublemakers* and LaBruce's *Boy, Girl* and *Bruce and Pepper Wayne Gacy's Home Movies*.

Source (edited): "http://en.wikipedia.org/wiki/J.D.s"

Jamming (fanzine)

Jamming! was a late 1970s to early 1980s UK punk zine edited by Tony Fletcher. Many of the early editions were printed and distributed by Better Badges.

Fletcher went on to become a successful music writer, with biographies of REM and Keith Moon to his name. He currently lives in upstate New York, blogs, and manages the band Radio 4.
Source (edited): "http://en.wikipedia.org/wiki/Jamming_(fanzine)"

KCDIY

KCDIY is a website that documents Kansas City, United States, Missouri's local punk music scene as well as other underground music and art scenes, as well as local activism. It includes a list of local events, venues, bands, and other local resources.

KCDIY is also the name of a music compilation featuring punk and hardcore bands from the Kansas City area such as Anxiety Attack, Crap Corps, Dick Cheney's Dick, The Hospital, Alert! Alert! The Skate -O Masochists, and many more.
Source (edited): "http://en.wikipedia.org/wiki/KCDIY"

Kill Your Pet Puppy

Kill Your Pet Puppy was a UK punkzine that ran for six issues between 1979 and 1984. It was edited by Tony Drayton (Tony D) who had previously produced Ripped and Torn fanzine, which he started in October 1976 and for 18 issues until 1979.

KYPP pushed the boundaries of punk through a period which saw the birth of anarcho-punk and the beginnings of the goth subculture. The final issue, No. 6, described a journey from a punk squat in London to Stonehenge Free Festival.

Groups featured in KYPP were Adam and the Ants, Crass, Bauhaus, Southern Death Cult, The Mob, The Associates, Charge, Sex Gang Children and the Cuddly Toys.

KYPP was written and designed in 'anarcho-situationist style' by a fluctuating group of around 12 members of the Puppy Collective. Influences on KYPP ranged from sixties undergrounds magazines like *OZ* and *International Times*, to Wilhelm Reich, the Angry Brigade, Aleister Crowley, surrealism, eco-feminism and David Bowie.

The Puppy Collective were also variously active participants in events and situations of the period - including a Sid Vicious Memorial March in 1979, the Wapping Autonomy Centre in 1981/2, Centro Iberico Anarchist Centre 1982, the 1982 Stonehenge to Greenham Peace Convoy and the 1983 Stop the City protest and the 1982/3/4 Stonehenge Free festivals.
Source (edited): "http://en.wikipedia.org/wiki/Kill_Your_Pet_Puppy"

Maximumrocknroll

MRR#1
Maximum Rocknroll Issue #1
Maximumrocknroll is a widely distributed, monthly not-for-profit fanzine based in San Francisco, USA. It features interviews, columns, and reviews from international contributors. Along with HearttattaCk and Punk Planet—who ceased publishing in 2006 and 2007 respectively—*Maximum RocknRoll* is considered by many to be one of the most important presences in punk, not only because of its wide-ranging coverage, but because it has been a constant and ideologically influential presence in the ever-changing punk community for three decades.

Maximum RocknRoll was an offshoot of a Berkeley punk radio show in the early 1980s, but it is in its zine form that *MRR* exerted its greatest influence and became as close to an institution as punk ideology allows. It was founded by Tim Yohannan in 1982 as the newsprint booklet in *Not So Quiet on the Western Front*, a compilation LP released on the then-Dead Kennedys' label Alternative Tentacles. The compilation included 47 Nevada and Northern California bands.

The first issues focused on more-local bands like musical and subcultural fixtures MDC. The coverage soon expanded to the entire continent and, by issue five, cover stories included features on Brazilian and Dutch underground punk. In the '80s, *MRR* was one of the very few US fanzines that insisted on the international scope of the punk movement, and strove to cover scenes around the world. Today the zine has surpassed its 300th issue, and continues to include international content and a strong political bent. As one of punk's largest zines, its reviews sections - *MRR* reviews records, demos and other fanzines - is one of the most comprehensive. It also reviews books, films, and videos.

Ethics

MRR has a large and dedicated all-volunteer staff. MRR reinforces the values of the punk underground by remaining independent and not-for-profit in contrast to the small number of the major media conglomerates which fund most mainstream artists. Every month, *MRR* publishes many submission-based band interviews. In addition, scene reports from across the globe keep the worldwide punk scene connected.

MRR has always had a policy of not giving coverage to, nor accepting advertising from, bands that record on major labels; that policy was soon extended to bands that are "produced and distributed" by or otherwise a subsidiary of a major label. For many years the magazine turned a large profit, but much of that money was "invested" into community projects, the most notable of which was probably the "Gilman Street Project", which created 924 Gilman Street, one of the world's most important and longest-lasting, punk rock clubs using a mostly volunteer staff (security are paid a percentage of each evening's door). *MRR* also directly sponsored The Epicenter Zone, a record store and show space in San Francisco. Furthermore, the zine gave thousands of dollars to other "projects" and clubs around the world.

Since Yohannan's 1998 death, the magazine has continued to operate on essentially the same economic principles. There have been eleven different content coordinators and two distribution coordinators in that time.

Writers

Over its years of publishing, *MRR* has featured a number of prominent writers, musicians, and personalities as columnists, such as Mykel Board, Jeff Bale, Chris Bickel, Jennifer Blowdryer, Anonymous Boy, Mike Bullshit, Eugene Chadbourne, Felix Havoc, Larry Livermore, Kent McClard, Nick Pell, Jack Rabid, Ben Weasel, Matt Wobensmith, Wells Tipley, George Tabb, Jen Angel, and editor Tim Yohannan. Its pages have served as the springboard for a wide variety of artists like Ted Rall and Dan Henk.

Criticism

The fact that *MRR* has become so large has not been without controversy; the zine has many critics on a number of issues. Editorial policy has sometimes been accused as narrow-minded or even elitist, causing some labels to boycott advertising in the zine or sending releases for review. The fact that punk is often considered as a movement opposed to authority and large institutions (see punk ideology) has also been an argument used to criticize the zine, which has sometimes been referred to as the 'Bible' of punk. This criticism spawned the creation of Punk Planet and HeartattaCk.

Musicians have also spoken out against the magazine. Jello Biafra claimed the magazine's criticism of him inspired people to assault him at a 1994 performance at 924 Gilman Street, though his assailants were not known to be affiliated with *MRR* in any way. He also claimed that their narrow definition of punk music amounts to a new form of political correctness. According to Biafra, "If 'Holiday in Cambodia' were released today, it would be banned from Maximum Rock N'Roll for not sounding punk." Jared Swilley, bassist in Atlanta punk band Black Lips, has criticized the magazine saying in an interview with *Clash* that it is the "most bullshit piece of fuck garbage poor excuse for a magazine ever. They're like: 'Oh, we want to keep everything 'authentic'…' And I'm like, fuck them! Don't use a computer, don't use a car, don't drink Coca-Cola. Move to a field, grow your own food." The song "MRR" by Fifteen criticizes Maximumrocknroll for petty articles and reviews and being "Big Brother's little brother".
Source (edited): "http://en.wikipedia.org/wiki/Maximumrocknroll"

No Cure

No Cure was a Newbury, UK based fanzine. It was part edited and produced by Richard Griffin and Richard Haworth with contributions from Jah P. The fanzine had a large interest in the Berkshire scene of the late 1970s and early 1980s and covered punk, Oi! post punk and Reggae. Many of the interviews were conducted by mailing a cassette and list of questions which resulted in some very interesting discussion's between band members without the problem of an interviewer butting in (see also cassette culture). Bands interviewed ranged from The Jam and Stiff Little Fingers to The Raincoats, Patrick Fitzgerald and The Instant Automatons. The photographer Pennie Smith was also interviewed. A thousand copies of No Cure were sold each issue and at one point it was the largest selling UK zine in New York.

Richard G later teamed up with Chris Green producing Bits fanzine and X Cassettes which released music from local bands like Quality Drivel. They were also involved in the promotion and distribution of a Reading area compilation LP *Beyond the River* released by Open Door records and featuring local bands such as Dig Dig Dig, El Seven, The Ballistics, The Erection Set, St Vitus Dance, Movita, Shrinking Men, A1 Vegetables, The Beating Hearts, Access and The Stills.

No Cure championed Berkshire bands such as The Lemon Kittens Infra Red Helicopters and the K-9s.

There was also an element of football firm banter, Richard G was a West Ham United fan and regularly squabbled in print with both contributors Sam Brown-artwork (Spurs) and readers supporting other London clubs.
Source (edited): "http://en.wikipedia.org/wiki/No_Cure"

Peroxide (punk zine)

Peroxide was a punk fanzine published and edited during the late 1970s by Andrew Thomas, Quentin Cook (AKA Norman Cook) and Ian McKay (AKA Ian Laidlaw). Inspired by punk zines such as Chainsaw, Peroxide lasted only two issues, with McKay being ousted by Cook after the first issue. Importantly however, the publication is noteworthy as it served to provide Cook with his first significant point of connection with the professional music business (his contact with Adam Ant being a notable example), and for both McKay and Thomas, their first experiences of publishing. Whilst Cook remained in the music business, McKay became a writer on the visual arts and culture, while Thomas moved into the business sector; he is currently the publisher of Communicate magazine and owner of Cravenhill Publishing.

Copies of Peroxide have latterly proved highly collectable owing largely to the connection with Norman Cook. Source (edited): "http://en.wikipedia.org/wiki/Peroxide_(punk_zine)"

Profane Existence

The Profane Existence Collective (referred to occasionally as 'P.E.') is a Minneapolis-based anarcho-punk collective. Established in 1989, the collective publishes a nationally-known zine (also called "Profane Existence"), as well as releasing and distributing anarcho-punk, crust, and grindcore music, and printing and publishing pamphlets and literature. Stacy Thompson describes the collective as "the largest, longest-lasting, and most influential collective in Anarcho-Punk so far." The collective folded in 1998, although its distribution arm, then called Blackened Distribution, continued operating. It restarted in 2000. "Making punk a threat again" is the group's slogan.

History

Launched in 1989, the Profane Existence magazine has been described as "the largest of the anarchist Punk fanzines in North America." The magazine deals with a very broad range of topics, including veganism, animal, women's and minority rights, anti-fascist action and the punk lifestyle. It publishes feature articles, interviews, reports on local scenes around the world, editorials, letters, "how-to" articles, and so on. Thompson writes that the zine "functions as [a newspaper] for many Anarcho-Punks, especially those in the Twin Cities area." Until it ceased publication in 1998 Profane Existence was free in the Twin Cities and cost $1–3 elsewhere; then as now customers who order the zine through the mail are only charged for shipping. The zine was initially published in a black and white tabloid format. It switched to an 8½ x 11" magazine format with issue #23 (Autumn 1994) but returned to a tabloid format (now with color front and back covers) with issue #38 (Spring 2000).

In 1992 the group copublished (with *Maximum Rock n Roll*) the first edition of *Book Your Own Fuckin' Life*, a directory (organized by region) of bands, distributors, venues, houses where "touring bands or traveling punks could sleep and sometimes eat for free," etc.--what Thompson describes as a "Yellow Pages of sorts" for "touring punk bands and punks in general."

Profane Existence Records, the collective's record label, was also founded in 1989. One of the label's first releases was "Extinction," the seminal New York City crust punk band Nausea's only full-length album, which John Griffin describes as "as important to the punks of the '90s as The Sex Pistols' *Never Mind the Bollocks* was to the punks of the late '70s." Another notable early release was Asbestosdeath's second 7", "Dejection"; Asbestosdeath's members went on to form the metal bands Sleep, High on Fire, and Om. Throughout the early and mid-1990s, Profane Existence released or distributed records by many other crust bands, including Doom, Misery, Fleas and Lice, Anarcrust, Counterblast, Dirt, and Hellbastard. Thompson writes that the label "became ground zero for [the crust] movement" and that the aesthetic of second-wave (i.e., beginning in the late 1980s) anarcho-punk "is currently exemplified by the bands released" on the label. More recently, the label has released music by bands like Behind Enemy Lines, MURDER DISCO X, Iskra, and The Cooters.

The collective is referenced by former Minnesotans The Hold Steady on their album "Separation Sunday" in the song "Stevie Nix", which contains the lyrics, "When we hit the Twin Cities, I didn't know that much about it / I knew Mary Tyler Moore and I knew Profane Existence."

Profane Existence Magazine Featured Artists

Profane Existence Magazine has regularly featured some of the most prominent punk visual artists in underground punk culture. The featured artists are known for illustrating punk album covers, magazines, showing their work in galleries or for their work as activists.

1. 58- "Hush" a.k.a. Jeremy Clark, best known for illustrating *Slug and Lettuce*.
2. 56 - Amy Toxic (illustrated for Alternative Tentacles, Toxic Narcotic, Caustic Christ, The Boston Phoenix,) Married to a member of Toxic Narcotic.
3. 55 – Matt Garabedian – (drummer and illustrator for Aus-Rotten and Behind Enemy Lines.)
4. 54- Fly a New York City artist and activist. (Book "Peops", illustrating Slug and Lettuce, mural at ABC No Rio.)
5. 48- "Steve" (From Visions of War, illustrated Profane Existence merchandise)
6. 47- Kieran Plunkett- (illustrated for UK Subs, The Restarts)
7. 46 – "Mid" aka Rob Middleton (illustrated for Napalm Death and Extreme Noise Terror)
8. 45- "Marald" (illustrated for Wartorn, Warcollapse, Imperial Leather, Borndead, State of Fear)

Source (edited): "http://en.wikipedia.org/wiki/Profane_Existence"

Punk (magazine)

PunkMagazine cover featuring the Ramones

PUNK magazine was a fanzine created by cartoonist John Holmstrom, publisher Ged Dunn and "resident punk" Legs McNeil in 1975. Its use of the term "punk rock," coined by writers for Creem magazine a few years earlier, led to its worldwide acceptance as the definition for the new bands that were producing a new sound based on the music of The Stooges, the New York Dolls, the MC5, and the Ramones. It was also the first publication to popularize the CBGB scene.

Punk published 15 issues between 1976 and 1979, as well as a special issue in 1981 (*The D.O.A. Filmbook*), and several more issues in the new millennium. Its covers featured Sex Pistols, Iggy Pop, Lou Reed, Patti Smith and Blondie.

Punk was a vehicle for examining the underground music scene in New York, and primarily for punk rock as found in clubs like CBGB, Zeppz, and Max's Kansas City. It mixed *Mad Magazine*-style cartooning by Holmstrom, Bobby London and a young Peter Bagge with the more straightforward pop journalism of the kind found in *Creem*. It also provided an outlet for female writers, artists and photographers who had been shut out of a male dominated underground publishing scene.

Punk magazine was home to (many of whom were being published for the first time) writers Mary Harron, Steve Taylor, Lester Bangs, Pam Brown, artists Buz Vaultz, Anya Phillips, and Screaming Mad George, and photographers Bob Gruen, Roberta Bayley and David Godlis. After Dunn left in early 1977 and McNeil quit shortly afterwards, Bruce Carleton (art director, 1977–1979), Ken Weiner (contributor, 1977–1979), and Elin Wilder, one of few African Americans involved in the early CBGB/punk rock scene, were added to the staff.

Punk was unsuccessfully restarted in 2001, shortly before 9/11. In 2006 the magazine was again revived, and new issues are still being published.

Source (edited): "http://en.wikipedia.org/wiki/Punk_(magazine)"

Punk Globe

Ginger Coyote, Publisher

Punk Globe, is a fanzine and online magazine, started by Ginger Coyote in July 1977. It was originally distributed on photocopied pages folded together. After its first year anniversary, Chris Coyle, manager for SVT, a San Francisco-based punk band, suggested a newsprint format. Ginger Coyote wrote on the website:

"We found Grant Printing--a company owned by the influential Fang Family, publishers of Asian Week and the San Francisco Independent *Community newspapers (and for a while, the* San Francisco Examiner*)--for the following 7 years. For our last 2 years, the magazine upgraded to heavier stock white paper printed at SF Litho."*

It was published as a fanzine until 1989, when Ginger Coyote started a band called White Trash Debutantes. The content of *Punk Globe* included a calendar of events, gossip, interviews, record reviews, photos, artwork, the Punk Of the Month Award and the humorous advice column, "Ask Sonny Bono." According to its publisher, "The magazine was lighthearted and a lot of fun... It became a hit, and in the last few years, 25,000 copies were being printed." The online version of *Punk Globe* surfaced in 2005, and contains some of the old content: articles, ads, artwork, photos and letters from past issues, as well as new artwork and photographs, gossip, news, interviews, CD, DVD, film and book reviews. Recent additions include an Internet forum and a Myspace page. According to Ginger Coyote, the website gets approximately 8,000 hits per day.

Punk Globe contributors included: Bebe Buell as associate editor and writer, Jello Biafra writing record reviews under the name "The Taste Police", Dorothy Lyman, Marc Floyd (AKA The Floydian Device), Robert Crumb, John Balano, Liz Derringer, Joe Jackson, Jon Gries, Lisa Zane, Matt Dillon, Ernie Townsend, Joe Dallesandro, Gerry-Jenn Wilson, Andrew Stevens, Judd Nelson, Lisa Booth, Sharla Cartner, Kim Acrylic, John Synder, Mark Arnold, Courtney Love, and Billy Gould.

Source (edited): "http://en.wikipedia.org/wiki/Punk_Globe"

Punk Planet

Punk Planet was a 16,000 print run punk zine, based in Chicago, Illinois, that focused most of its energy on looking at punk subculture rather than punk as simply another genre of music to which teenagers listen. In addition to covering music, *Punk Planet* also covered visual arts and a wide variety of progressive issues — including media criticism, feminism, and labor issues. The most notable features in *Punk Planet* were the interviews and album reviews. The interviews generally ran two or three pages, and tended to focus on the motivations of the artist (or organizer, activist, or whoever) being interviewed. *Punk Planet* tried to review nearly all the records it received, so long as the record label wasn't owned or partially owned by a major label. This led to a review section typically longer than thirty pages, covering a variety of musical styles. Although much of the music thus reviewed was, expectedly, aggressive rock, the reviews also covered country, folk, hip-hop, indie rock, and other genres. The Punk Planet reviews section also encompassed independently released comics, zines, and DVDs. A number of poor distribution deals and the collapse of IndyMedia resulted in mounting debts for the editors. As a result, issue 80 was shipped with a cover reading: "This is the final issue of Punk Planet, after this the fight is yours." Subsidiary business Punk Planet books remains in business.

Notable issue topics/subjects

- Issue 22 — first issue with full color, cardstock cover
- Issues 24, 46, and 67: *Art & Design 1, 2,* and *3* — theme issue
- Issue 34 — first issue with perfect binding
- Issue 50: *The Chicago Issue* — theme issue
- Issue 55 and 75: *The Revenge of Print 1* and *2* — theme issue
- Issue 80: final issue

History and other projects

The first issue of the zine was published in May 1994, in part as a response to the perception that *Maximum Rock and Roll* was becoming too elitist. In September 2006, *Punk Planet* had printed 75 issues of their bi-monthly publication, and in the fall of 2004 launched a book publishing arm, Punk Planet Books, in conjunction with the New York-based small press Akashic Books. Punk Planet Books has published four titles as of May 2006: "Hairstyles of the Damned" by Joe Meno (August 2004, ISBN 1-888451-70-X), "All the Power: Revolution Without Illusion" by Mark Andersen (September 2004, ISBN 1-888451-72-6), "Lessons in Taxidermy" by Bee Lavender (March 2005)(ISBN 1-888451-79-3), and "100 Posters, 134 Squirrels" by Jay Ryan (November 2005, ISBN 1-888451-93-9).

In September 2006, Punk Planet partnered with the website, ZineWiki, to publish, online, exclusive articles from past print issues.

On June 18, 2007, a post at www.punkplanet.com informed the public that after 13 years and 80 issues, Punk Planet's final issue was being sent out. The reasoning pointed to "bad distribution deals, disappearing advertisers, and a decreasing audience of subscribers."

As a result, editor Daniel Sinker decided to place his focus on the online website, but it has since gone offline. In its place is a statement, "This is it, folks. The Punk Planet website is closed. Two years after the closure of the magazine, it just seemed time."

Criticism

Like the other big national US fanzine — *Maximum Rock and Roll* — *Punk Planet* was not without its detractors. Many complained about its high price, perfect binding, and a perceived over-attention to layout and style (such as the inclusion of page numbers and a table of contents), which had to a certain extent moved it away from the traditional punk aesthetic.

Source (edited): "http://en.wikipedia.org/wiki/Punk_Planet"

Punk zine

A **punk zine** (or **punkzine**) is a zine devoted to punk culture, most often punk rock music, bands, or the DIY punk ethic. Punk zines are the most likely place to find punk literature.

Selection of British and American punk zines, 1994-2004

One of the earliest punk zines was the New York magazine *Punk*. It was started by John Holmstrom, Ged Dunn, and Legs McNeil, who published the first issue in January 1976. The zine championed the early New York underground music scene and helped associate the word "punk" with these bands, most notably, The Ramones. *Punk* received a flash of attention in England until 1977 when the punks across the Atlantic started making their own punk zines.

An early UK punk zine was *Sniffin'*

Glue, produced by Mark Perry, who also founded the band Alternative TV, in 1976. However, the magazine never applied this term to itself, and indeed it is thought that it did not come into use until the early 1980s. The term *punkzine* was possibly coined amongst anarcho-punk circles, specifically by writers who objected to the connotations of the word *fanzine*, believing the first part of the word to imply the slavish following of pop groups, and unquestioning acceptance of celebrity culture.

The DIY aesthetic of punk created a thriving underground press; someone could not only start a band but also be a music journalist and critic. Mark Perry produced the first photocopied issue of *Sniffin' Glue* in London immediately after that Ramones concert in 1976. In the US, such titles as *Punk, Search & Destroy* (later REsearch), *Flipside* and *Slash* chronicled and helped to define the emerging culture. Such amateur magazines took inspiration from the rock fanzines of the early 70s, which themselves had roots in the science fiction fan community. Probably the most influential of the fanzines to cross over from SF fandom to rock and, later, punk rock and "new wave" was Greg Shaw's *Who Put the Bomp,* published since 1970. Punk zines were produced in many European countries in the years after the first productions for example the first appeared in Ireland in March 1977.

The politically-charged *Maximum RocknRoll* and the anarchist *Profane Existence* were among the most important fanzines in the 1980s and onward. By that time, every local "scene" had at least one, often primitively- or casually-published magazine with news, gossip, and interviews with local or touring bands. The magazine *Factsheet Five* chronicled thousands of underground publications and "zines" in the 1980s and 1990s.

List of punk fanzines and punkzines

- *Absolutely Zippo*
- *Artcore* Cardiff, 1986-
- *Black Market Magazine* San Diego, 1985-1995
- *Burnt Offering* Northampton, England, 1979 - 1980
- *Chainsaw* Croydon, England, 1977-1984
- *Cometbus*
- *Fracture*
- *Flipside* — Los Angeles, 1977-2000
- *HeartattaCk*
- *Homocore* (San Francisco, California, 1988-1991)
- *Jamming*
- *J.D.s*
- *KCDIY*
- *Kill Your Pet Puppy*
- *Maximum RocknRoll*
- *New York Rocker*
- *No Cure*
- *Profane Existence* Minneapolis, 1989-present
- *Punk Magazine* New York, 1976-1979
- *Rancid News* - UK, 2003 (now called Last Hours)
- *Razorcake*
- *RE/Search*
- *Search and Destroy* - San Francisco, 1977
- *Short, Fast & Loud*
- *Slash* - Los Angeles, 1977-1980
- *Slug and Lettuce*
- *Sluggo!*, Austin, Texas, 1978-?
- *Sniffin' Glue* — UK, 1976-1977
- *Sticky Paste Is Good To Eat*
- *Suburban Voice*
- *TNSrecords Fanzine* - UK, (relaunched) 2008 - present
- *Under the Volcano*
- *KAOS*- italian punk zine, 2005, present

Source (edited): "http://en.wikipedia.org/wiki/Punk_zine"

Razorcake

Razorcake is a 501(c)(3) non-profit organization that publishes the Razorcake fanzine, a DIY punk rock fanzine published bi-monthly out of Los Angeles, California. It was co-founded by Todd Taylor (former Flipside managing editor) and Sean Carswell (author and Gorsky Press co-founder) in 2001.

History

As Flipside was going under, Taylor decided that he did not want to cease to write about music. His initial idea was to create a webzine instead of a print zine because of financial restraints. Taylor told Carswell, during a trip to Florida, about his plan for a webzine. Carswell suggested that a print edition be produced. Taylor concurred, stipulating that Carswell needed move to Los Angeles in order to assist with the production of the fanzine.

The name for both editions was chosen while searching for a domain name. Many of the 300 possibilities, such as "Born to Rock" and "Barbed Wire Asshole," were either taken, too expensive, or thought to be a name that "would trap [them]." "Razorcake" was suggested by Katy (a.k.a. KT), a friend of Taylor and Carswell. The name was chosen since it meant nothing and was economical, and Skinny Dan (a.k.a. Danny) set up the website at www.razorcake.com.

March 2001 saw the first issue of the print edition of Razorcake. The inaugural issue was the only one to bear a newsprint cover. Every issue since the first has had a glossy cover. As opposed to the cover, the focus of the content within Razorcake has never changed. Also, the fanzine's circulation has more than doubled (to 6,000) since the first issue.

Non-Profit Status

In late 2005, Razorcake was approved by the IRS as an official 501(c)(3) non-profit organization. Razorcake is the first magazine in America dedicated to independent music to obtain 501(c)(3) status. The new organization combined the Gorsky Press and the zine, and is now officially called Razorcake/Gorsky Press, Inc. This meant that not one person could individually benefit from Razorcake. All money earned goes back into day-to-day operations and keeping Razorcake afloat. Razorcake wanted to show that its business model was out in the open in order to demonstrate that a sustainable business could be ethical, fair, and true to its ideals long after its first issue.

Ethics

From the interviews it runs (contributors interview bands based solely on their appreciation), to the advertising allowed (no major labels and "below-market price" advertising to those in the DIY community), to the method of the zine's distribution (not via chain stores, but directly to individual stores and people), Razorcake operates outside of the corporate structures that a traditional music magazine would embrace. With only two people on staff, all of the material offered in both editions of Razorcake is donated.

Content

Razorcake sees itself as a constant celebration and criticism of contemporary DIY punk rock. Every piece that Razorcake runs is exclusive. Razorcake provides long-format, detailed interviews with contemporary punk bands (including Dan Padilla, Toys That Kill, Fucked Up, Shang-A-Lang, The Ergs!) and with punk pioneers (such as The Adolescents, Dead Moon, TSOL), with an ongoing attention to its own roots of East Los Angeles (publication of the East L.A. Family Tree, and including interviews with The Brat, Alice Bag, Los Illegals, and Circle One). Razorcake not only interviews bands from all over the globe (Gorilla Angreb, Career Suicide, The Regulations), but punk-affiliated artists—photographers (Edward Colver, Bev Davies), graphic designers (Diane Gamboa, John E. Miner), writers (Brad Warner, Chris Walter)—and political thinkers such as Howard Zinn, Christian Parenti, Noam Chomsky, and Candace Falk and Gary Pateman (curators of the Emma Goldman Paper Project).

Contributors

Besides Todd Taylor and Sean Carswell, former Flipside writers Donofthedead, Jimmy Alvarado, Designated Dale, Kat Jetson, The Rhythm Chicken, Jessica T., Nardwuar the Human Serviette, and Rich Mackin all wrote for the premier issue. Many of them remain with the publication, but Razorcake also has a raft of columnists who are well known in the DIY punk rock community as zinesters, musicians, and artists including Ben Snakepit, Amy Adoyzie, Rev. Nørb, Maddy Tight Pants, Dan Monick, Jim Ruland, Liz O., Kiyoshi Nakazawa, and Mitch Clem. In addition to these columnists, Razorcake has one staff member, Daryl, several dedicated reviewers, and guest contributors.

Gorsky Press

Gorsky Press, the book publishing arm of Razorcake, founded by Sean Carswell and Felizon Vidad, predated both the Razorcake website and zine. Its mission is similar to Razorcake in that it focuses on high quality material from marginalized and disenfranchised writers. Gorsky Press has released books by underground writers such as Patricia Geary, Bucky Sinister, James Jay, and Jennifer Whiteford.
Source (edited): "http://en.wikipedia.org/wiki/Razorcake"

Rolling Thunder (journal)

Rolling Thunder is a biannual "anarchist journal of dangerous living" published by anarchist collective CrimethInc. since the Summer of 2005. It is our attempt to offer a wild-eyed, fire-breathing, militant periodical
that can cover the adventures of a dissident high school student skipping class as easily as a street riot that sets an embassy aflame:
that neither reduces the organic impulses of revolt to inert theory
nor prioritizes conventional activism over the subversive elements present in every other walk of life
but instead focuses on sharing the stories of those who step out of line
(that is, of all of us, in our finest moments)
and sharing the skills developed in the process
(not to mention the poetry)
so that many more may do so
and do so more boldly
and so that liberty and community and all those other beautiful things
may triumph.
—*CrimethInc.*
In a review of Issue 5, *Last Hours* praised the magazine for presenting "some of the best critical analysis of the anarchist movement both in the United States and in Europe ... in recent years".
Source (edited): "http://en.wikipedia.org/wiki/Rolling_Thunder_(journal)"

Slash (fanzine)

Slash was a punk rock-related fanzine published in the United States from 1977 to 1980.

The magazine was a large-format tabloid focused on the Los Angeles punk scene, though it did not restrict itself to local acts: its first cover featured Dave Vanian of The Damned. It regularly covered such L.A. bands as The Screamers, The Skulls, Nervous Gender and X. With relatively wide distribution for a punk zine, Slash helped bring the L.A. underground scene to the attention of the rest of the world. At the same time, in featuring articles and reviews on reggae, blues, and rockabilly, it introduced punk audiences to a wide range of then-unfamiliar musical genres. Writers Claude "Kickboy Face" Bessy, Craig Lee, Richard Meltzer, Jeffrey Lee Pierce, Chris D. and Pleasant Gehman, and cartoonist Gary Panter were among the major contributors. Photo contributors included David Arnoff, Susan Carson, Kerry Colonna, Ed Colver, Diane Gamboa, Frank Gargani, Jenny Lens, Melanie Nissen, Donna Santisi, Ann Summa, Scott Lindgren, and coeditor Philomena Winstanley.

The fanzine also gave birth to Slash Records, an important punk record label. Slash magazine folded in 1980, as many of the main principals involved were increasingly concentrating on other activities. Bob Biggs was more involved in running the label; many of the writers were concentrating on their own musical activities. In addition, there was a widespread perception that punk rock was dying, as movements such as post-punk, hardcore, and deathrock were emerging while many of the original Los Angeles punk bands (such as The Germs and The Weirdos) were breaking up, and in such a changing environment Slash had essentially served its purpose.

Complete List of Issues

- Vol. 1 #1 May 1977. Cover: Dave Vanian (The Damned) photo by Melanie Nissen
- Vol. 1 #2 June 1977. Cover: John Denney (The Weirdos) photo by Melanie Nissen
- Vol. 1 #3 Aug. 1977. Cover: Johnny Rotten (Sex Pistols)
- Vol. 1 #4 Sept. 1977. Cover: Kerry Colonna (live collage) photo by Philomena Winstanley
- Vol. 1 #5 Oct. 1977. Cover: Debbie Harry (Blondie)
- Vol. 1 #6 Dec. 1977. Cover: Exene Cervenka (X)
- Vol. 1 #7 Jan 1978. Cover: Local Scene Makers
- Vol. 1 #8 Feb. 1978. Cover: Poly Styrene (X-Ray Spex) photo by Virginia Turbett
- Vol. 1 #9 April 1978. Cover: Bobby Pyn/Darby Crash
- Vol. 1 #10 May 1978. Cover: Alice Bag (The Bags)
- Unnumbered One Year Anniversary Issue. Free, No date or volume number. Cover: Collage of prior issue covers.
- Vol. 1 #11 July 1978. Cover: Spazz Attack
- Vol. 1 #12 Aug. 1978. Cover: The Screamers photo by Melanie Nissen
- Vol. 2 #1 Sept. 1978. Cover: Pete Tosh
- Vol. 2 #2 Nov. 1978. Cover: Siouxsie & the Banshees photo by Stevenson
- Vol. 2 #3 Jan. 1979. Cover: Drawing by John Van Hamersveld
- Vol. 2 #4 March 1979. Cover: The Cramps photo by Melanie Nissen
- Vol. 2 #5 May 1979. Cover: Rasta illustration by Rick Monzon
- Vol. 2 #6 June 1979. Cover: Alleycats photo by Melanie Nissen
- Vol. 2 #7 Aug. 1979. Cover: Drawing of "Jimbo" by Gary Panter
- Vol. 2 #8 Sept. 1979. Cover: David Thomas (Pere Ubu) photo by Melanie Nissen
- Vol. 2 #9 Oct. 1979. Cover: Su Tissue (Suburban Lawns) illustration by Mark Vallen
- Vol. 2 #10 Nov. 1979. Cover: David Byrne (Talking Heads) photo by Kerry Colonna
- Vol. 2 #11 Dec. 1979. Cover: James Chance illustration by Mike Fink
- Vol. 3 #1 Jan/Feb. 1980. Cover: Lee Ving (Fear)
- Vol. 3 #2 Mar. 1980. Cover: Winston Rodney (Burning Spear) photo by Scott Lindgren
- Vol. 3 #2 April. 1980. Cover: Malcolm McLaren and Johnny Rotten illustration by Bob Biggs
- Vol. 3 #3 May 1980. Cover: Johanna Went
- Vol. 3 #5 (Final Issue) Summer 1980. Cover: Hardcore punk illustration by Mark Vallen

Source (edited): "http://en.wikipedia.org/wiki/Slash_(fanzine)"

Slug and Lettuce (fanzine)

Slug and Lettuce is a free newsprint punk zine started in New York City and currently based in Richmond, Virginia. Its byline reads "A zine supporting the Do-It-Yourself ethics of the punk community". It is published quarterly and in spring 2007, it will be twenty years old. It is edited by Christine Boarts Larson, who also writes a column for Maximum Rocknroll and runs a book distribution business. She describes her zine as "providing space for communication and networking within underground music and political scenes" and states that "it was through her zine that she forged connections to the larger underground scene which gave her the 'inspiration and dedication' to chart a course for herself outside the mainstream" (quoted in *Notes from Underground: Zines and the Politics of Alternative Culture*).

Contents

Each issue contains columns with DIY/anarcho-punk themes pertaining to anti-authoritarian politics, vegetarian/vegan action, radical parenting, DIY culture, gardening and activism generally. *Slug and Lettuce* also features zine, book, and record reviews and Christine Boarts-Larson's band photography.

Slug and Lettuce has featured the comic Zero Content by Fly, the Folk Punk art of Jeremy Clark and the Medieval Punk art of Sean Aaberg.

Recent news

In issue number 89 in autumn 2006, Christine Boarts Larson announces that issue 90 will be the twentieth anniversary issue. It is postponed to May 2007 owing to her pregnancy. The 20th anniversary issue - #90 came out in the fall of 2007. It is still available.

Contact

Slug and Lettuce can be reached at PO Box 26632 Richmond, VA 23261-6632. Zines are free in person or sent out for the cost of postage.

Source (edited): "http://en.wikipedia.org/wiki/Slug_and_Lettuce_(fanzine)"

Sluggo!

Sluggo! was a pioneering Austin, Texas fanzine covering the late 1970s Punk rock/New Wave music scene. Founded in 1978 by Nick West and E.A. Srere, Sluggo! began as a tabloid-sized photocopied publication, and evolved into a quintessential DIY publication. With the donation of a Multilith 1250 offset press and an array of colored inks, Sluggo! acquired its distinctive multi-colored, multi-faceted appearance. Sluggo! look was also defined by its unique covers – hand-crafted on some issues, individually silk-screened on black velvet on the finale.

The early issues centered primarily on music with reviews of shows of both local and touring bands, and record reviews of both national and international acts such as Pere Ubu, PIL, Throbbing Gristle. In addition to music, Sluggo! columnists also held forth on subjects ranging from religion to science, international politics to local gossip.

In 1979, Sluggo! departed from the typical music fanzine with the introduction of its thematic issues. Topics were Violence, Unco, and culminated with its "*Industrial Collapse*" issue. Sluggo! also created the Instant Review, publishing critiques of local performances overnight with free distribution on the streets the very next day. The Sluggo! press was used not only for printing the fanzine but was also made available to local bands for printing band posters and record covers, and to other raconteurs for printing various handbills and broadsides. Sluggo! House became one of the epicenters of the exploding Austin scene and drew considerable local and national attention as a hotbed of musical and artistic action.

Sluggo! provided inspiration to other writers and entrepreneurs to found and publish their own fanzines including Xiphoid Process and Contempo Culture from Austin, and a myriad of others throughout Texas. Sluggo!'s topical format also served as a model to the staff at Search & Destroy Magazine from San Francisco to expand their horizons and begin the RE/Search magazine with issues devoted to a single topic.

Sluggo! was a primary ambassador of the 1970s Austin Punk/New Wave scene throughout Texas, the nation and overseas. Its evolution from a modest home grown fanzine to a distinctively quirky journal with ambitions of a wider cultural window mirrors the peculiar growth of the Austin punk music and artistic scene, and its future development into the behemoth it is today.

Source (edited): "http://en.wikipedia.org/wiki/Sluggo!"

Sniffin' Glue

Sniffin' Glue is the name of a monthly punk zine started by Mark Perry in July 1976 and released for about a year. The name is derived from a Ramones song "Now I Wanna Sniff Some Glue." Others that wrote for the magazine that later became well known journalists include Danny Baker.

Although initial issues only sold 50 copies, circulation soon increased to 15,000. The innovative appeal of Sniffin' Glue was its immediacy.

Sniffin' Glue was not so much badly written as barely written; grammar was non-existent, layout was haphazard, headlines were usually just written in felt tip, swearwords were often used in lieu of a reasoned argument. . .all of which gave Sniffin' Glue its urgency and relevance.

The early days of the punk movement largely failed to attract the entrance of television or the mainstream press, and Sniffin' Glue remains a key source of photographs of, and information about, contributors to the scene.

NME acclaimed "Sniffin' Glue" as "the nastiest, healthiest and funniest piece of press in the history of rock'n'roll habits" and it really became the true chronicle of the early days of British punk rock as well as pioneering the DIY punk ethic. Later, some called it the Bible of the punk movement. For the final issue Mark's sidekick Sniffin' Glue photographer, business affairs and later band manager Harry Murlowski recorded Love Lies Limp released as a flexi disc record - the first release from Mark Perry's band Alternative TV.

Fearing absorption into the mainstream music press, Perry ceased publication in 1977. In the last issues he encouraged his readers to follow him with their own punk fanzines.

"Sniffin' Glue" is often incorrectly credited as the source of the illustration featuring drawings of three chord shapes, captioned, "this is a chord, this is another, this is a third. Now form a band", this drawing actually originally appeared in December 1976 in another fanzine 'Sideburns' and was later reproduced in the Stranglers fanzine 'Strangled'

In 2000, Mark Perry published *Sniffin' Glue: The Essential Punk Accessory*, which is a compilation of all the issues of the fanzine with some new material written by him. Sniffin' Glue is referenced in the song "Three Sevens Clash" by The Alarm, a tribute to 1977, and a follow on from their previous punk tribute "45 RPM".

Source (edited): "http://en.wikipedia.org/wiki/Sniffin%27_Glue"

Suburban Voice

Suburban Voice is a punk zine published by Al Quint. Originally started in 1982, it was titled *Suburban Punk* for the first 10 issues, and then the titled changed to *Suburban Voice*. Although the zine has other contributors, Al is the primary writer for most of the material. The zine is noted for its in-depth interviews and detailed music reviews.
Source (edited): "http://en.wikipedia.org/wiki/Suburban_Voice"

The Positives

The Positives (Os Positivos) was a Portuguese comics fanzine drawn by Valter de Matos that run through the years 1997 and 1998 before folding. It exists now mostly on its web form as a webcomic.

File:OsPositivos.jpg
155px

Plot Summary

The main series, known as "XXX-Irritant", followed the day-to-day adventures of Xavier and friends until his suicide in the final volume. Although the end of their adventures is known, mainly because the last published volume has a flash back narrative that slowly unveils events, the final issue was never made public and since then Xavier has appeared in many short stories of the Positives universe, supposedly taking place before the events of that last number.

Animal Rights, Autobiographical Side And Artwork

The Positives (also known as "P+") started off as a vehicle of animal rights and direct action awareness, but soon turned into another autobiographical comic that relate back to the sixties underground comix tradition.

Using as their own motto "true undergroung comix", P+ is drawn with a punk D.I.Y. attitude, and the quality of their artwork is definitely not the main concern, although throughout their existence there's a visible evolution of style, until it became a recognizable format: simple black outlines with no shades or fills drawn on cheaper paper. The Positives have a remarkable poor layout in terms of comic language, but the author has justified those transgressions with "at the speed at which the characters talk to me I can't concern myself with small things like continuity" . One particular feature in P+ is the absence of eyes on their characters, an important asset to any comic as a mean of expression, but one which P+ manages to survive without.

Story Line

If the artwork got the backseat, the story line is definitely driving the P+ forward. Written on a very offensive language to say the least, the street tone at which the characters spoke set the pace to one of the most candid comics at the time, pulling the reader into the story, which revolved around the Xavier's love for Susana.

The P+ also has a second story line: from time to time, the reader is pulled away of Xavier and friends adventures only to find himself on a television studio were those events are being recorded. In this sudden new reality, most characters have a very different personality than the one they are performing for the camera and the rest od the P+ cast is introduced.

Some of the Characters

Xavier - plays the hero on P+, it's a very obnoxious person off-camera.

Susana - depicted as a very sweet and angelical person, its performed by the only professional actress on P+, a famous porn star looking for a more arty career.

Director (also known as Dictator) - tries to film his masterpiece against the accidental sabotages of his own cast of amateurs.

Shark (the only non-human character)- the greedy lawyer and producer whose schemes to make money out of the P+ tend to provoke Director's anger.

Animal - a reincarnation of a younger Director that shows up on stage only to further annoy him with accusations of selling out to the system. To further complicate the P+ story line, sometimes Animal enters the "filmed" adventures of Xavier and friends as himself, against Director's willing (who tends to cut the scenes when it happens).
Source (edited): "http://en.wikipedia.org/wiki/The_Positives"

Touch and Go: The Complete Hardcore Punk Zine '79-'83"

Touch and Go: The Complete Hardcore Punk Zine '79-'83 is a 576-page trade paperback book containing all 22 issues of the Touch and Go Punk zine, a punk magazine that chronicled the early hardcore punk and post punk scenes.

The book consists of the writings of Tesco Vee and Dave Stimson - the founders and designers of the Touch and Go zine - which eventually evolved into Touch and Go Records, owned by Corey Rusk. The book contains many forewords and introductions written by Tesco Vee, Dave Stimson, Steve Miller, Henry Rollins, Keith Morris, Peter Davis, Henry Owings, Byron Coley, Corey Rusk, John Brannon, and Ian MacKaye.

The zine, which is chronicled in the book, contains early reviews and features on bands like Black Flag, Circle Jerks, Wire (band), Minor Threat, Teen Idles, The Necros, Gang of Four, among others.

The book was released on June 30, 2010. It was published by Bazillion Points Publishing. The ISBN is 978-0979616389.

Source (edited): "http://en.wikipedia.org/wiki/Touch_and_Go:_The_Complete_Hardcore_Punk_Zine_%2779-%2783%22"

Verbicide Magazine

Verbicide is an independent entertainment website based jointly out of Ludlow, Vermont and Brooklyn, New York. It is co-published via Scissor Press by founding editor Jackson Ellis and creative director Nathaniel Pollard.

Verbicide was founded in 1999 in New Haven, Connecticut by Jackson Ellis. The first issue came out in September 1999, a handmade (cut-and-paste), 12-page photocopied zine. By 2003, Verbicide was a full-color offset quarterly with a glossy cover, with free circulation in New York, Austin, Los Angeles, Boston, and San Francisco, and newsstand circulation in all 50 states and Canada.

In March 2009, the 25th and final print edition of Verbicide was released, and the magazine was relaunched online on August 1, 2009. Upon moving online, Heather Schofner became the features editor, and Erin Gambrill joined as the fiction editor.

Verbicide includes music reviews, interviews with musicians and authors, book and film reviews, and featured columns by Larry Livermore, Mark Huddle, and Douglas Novielli. Past features have featured interviews with the likes of Chuck D, Henry Rollins, Ian MacKaye, Saul Williams, The Gorillaz, The Donnas, and the Beastie Boys. Verbicide has published fiction by authors including Raegan Butcher, Jeremy Robert Johnson, Diane DiPrima, Christopher Staley, Nelson Algren, John Fante, Joe Meno, and Jack Kerouac.

Los Angeles zine Razorcake described Verbicide as a "a good mag by an editor who's fighting the good fight". Source (edited): "http://en.wikipedia.org/wiki/Verbicide_Magazine"